A FAILURE'S REMINISCENCE

LESSONS FROM A LIFETIME OF MANAGEMENT BLUNDERS

Narendra KV

Preface
Mr. Venkatraman Balakrishnan
Venture Capitalist & Ex CFO, Infosys Limited

Rezorce Research Foundation
A Not – For – Profit Trust Dedicated to Governance & Performance

Rezorce Research Foundation
A Not – For – Profit Trust Dedicated to Indology

111/1 II Floor VI Main VIII Cross Malleswaram Bangalore 560003 India
www.rezorce.com | +91 9243046271 | narendra.kv@rezorce.com

Global Rights reserved by Author

$25.00 | £18.57 | €22.24
$4.00 | Rs.299 | £2.97 | €3.56 - EBook
$12.00 – Soft Copy

ISBN-13: 9798408599028 [Hard Cover]
ASIN: B09QFZ4W1W
ISBN: 9798408831081 [Soft Copy]
BISAC: Management

All rights are reserved. No part of this publication may be reproduced, stored in a retrieval system or transmitted in any form or by any means without the prior written permission of Rezorce Research Foundation or as expressly permitted by law or under the terms agreed with the appropriate reprographic rights organization. Enquiries concerning reproduction outside the scope of the above should be sent to Rezorce Research Foundation at the above address

You must not circulate this book in any other binding or cover and you must impose the same condition of any acquirer

Printed and Published by Rezorce Research Foundation, Bangalore, India

DEDICATED TO

ALL MANAGERS WHO TRY & FAIL

ALSO

TO ALL OTHER MANAGERS WHO DON'T
ACT FEARING FAILURE

Thanks to my family who are my pillar of support

A FAILURE'S REMINISCENCE
LESSONS FROM A LIFETIME OF MANAGEMENT BLUNDERS

INTRODUCTION

In my long management experience, I have seen more failures than success. From 1994, when I started my first software company, I have got opportunities to work across the globe and in many challenging circumstances. I have changed my domain and specialization every five years. I have sold power management products; done energy audits; built software products; architected and managed extremely large, public sector software roll – outs; managed global staffing operations; ran virtual companies; edited science magazines; managed innovation led businesses and in between ran visible, non – governmental organizations with some success [and more failures].

My cumulative experience has given me insight to many stupid mistakes that I have made over time. Once we leave behind a mess and move ahead in life, it becomes easy to reflect on the issues involved. On hindsight, every mistake appears so obvious. When you analyze the same situation from an "outsider – insider" perspective, you realize that the failure was logical and designed to happen. Away from the heat of the battle, the same set of data points provides a different perspective and a whole new solution path that could have saved the situation.

As I interact with entrepreneurs and business executives every day, I see much of the same mistakes I have made being repeated

A FAILURE'S REMINISCENCE
LESSONS FROM A LIFETIME OF MANAGEMENT BLUNDERS

everywhere. The same fads return, and same jargons are bandied – the results are equally predictable.

In the beginning, I told myself that my capacity to blunder was something unimaginable. I have lost so often that I do not believe I can succeed without a few failures. I have seen people become cynical with failure, but my conditioning has made me expect and accept failure as a natural part of the process. Being kicked around ceaselessly for over two decades has meant that I have started to love the kicks and look forward to them as a part of my daily routine.

The process has not made me a billionaire, buy a BMW, build a palace, enjoy weekends on my farm or get me closer to political power or influential position or awards. The failures have only helped me stand firm on the ground and reflect ceaselessly.

The birth of my daughter and my painful realization that I lost out seeing my son grow, made me step out of the executive rat race. Standing back and observing the scene made a huge difference to my perception about success and failures.

I gradually realized the reason kings regarded sages highly. While I was continuously blundering in my own business, I could clearly

A FAILURE'S REMINISCENCE
LESSONS FROM A LIFETIME OF MANAGEMENT BLUNDERS

see what mistakes others were doing. This was because I had done all those mistakes earlier and seen the consequences firsthand.

I have a habit of recording my meetings in notebooks. All the mistakes are recorded in these notebooks. Each time I revisit old notebooks, I notice that there was a pattern to the mistakes. This book is all about common failures that executives make and is seldom spoken about in management classes. I write this book, to let others like me know that they are not the only ones making stupid mistakes. We are a pack that complement each other and seldom speak.

I penned my thoughts over a five-year period. The purpose was not so much to publish, but more as a record of my personal learnings from each encounter.

Every essay is a contra – view to popular and accepted principles. It is not anyone's case that I am right in every aspect. I wish the thoughts would provoke readers to think and contemplate on alternatives. In my view, that is the ultimate purpose of any book.

If management students can debate and spend time on each of these experiences, there is a world to explore. I urge groups to discuss the logical solutions that their textbooks instruct, and their revered teachers explain and compare my experiences. It would make their time in colleges more interesting

A FAILURE'S REMINISCENCE
LESSONS FROM A LIFETIME OF MANAGEMENT BLUNDERS

PREFACE

Winston Churchill said, "**Success is the ability to go from failure to failure without losing your enthusiasm**"

We always wonder why United States is so successful economically. It is one of the most productive economies in the world that respects merit thereby attracting the best talent. More than all these attributes, it is also an economy that allows failure without any stigma attached to it. It provides a perfect ecosystem of risk capital, human resources, research and innovation for an entrepreneur to thrive and succeed. It is that ecosystem which applauds failure and encourages entrepreneurs to take risks that makes United States the most innovative economy in the world.

Successful entrepreneurs are those who had failed couple of times earlier. The beauty is to treat every failure as a step to success, learn from the mistakes and passionately pursue one's dreams. It is a common view that success comes through rapidly fixing our mistakes rather than getting things right the first time. Also "success" is the biggest impediment to

A FAILURE'S REMINISCENCE
LESSONS FROM A LIFETIME OF MANAGEMENT BLUNDERS

succeed. If you are successful, your ability to take risks and change the status quo is very limited. You are afraid of the failure when you change the status quo. Great organizations which are successful fade away when the entrepreneur's ability to take risks goes away.

Becoming a successful entrepreneur is an interesting journey. You have an idea, you get a set of like-minded people together, and you put your own money and build on that idea. The family may or may not support due to unpredictability of earnings. You build out the idea and then figure out that the market has changed. You pivot the start-up and change focus. Raising money is another experience. It is both humbling and rewarding. Raising money is one thing but getting connected to the ecosystem is another. Once you raise money, you have to play by the rules as there is an outside investor. There will be continuous pressure to deliver. Also, understanding the financial nuances and understanding the value of equity while at the same time have enough skin in the game is another experience. Managing the existing talent and attracting the best talent will be challenging. If you surmount all these and finally succeed, it is like conquering the Everest. There is lot of sweat and blood behind every success. The moment of truth comes when there is an exit either in the form of a buyout or an IPO.

Many start-ups fail and very few succeeds. The world only sees the success stories but largely ignores the one's that failed. In the Venture Capital world, behind every successful start-up there are at least ten other failed companies. The common trait of a failed company is the lack of mentorship and guidance. An entrepreneur needs to be a multi-faceted person. But, in reality, he will be a technology or businessperson. You need someone who had seen through all and guide you and mentor you through the journey. You need someone who can navigate through the difficulties and show you the path to success. Having a set of good

A FAILURE'S REMINISCENCE
LESSONS FROM A LIFETIME OF MANAGEMENT BLUNDERS

advisors and mentors is one of the key elements to success for a startup company.

The book "A Failure's Reminiscence" by Narendra KV fills that gap. This book is a compendium of various experiences the author had gone through in his professional journey and makes an interesting reading. Very often we do not realize the mistakes we make during our professional career. But, when we reminiscence it at a later point of time dispassionately, we do understand that an alternate point of view was possible and gain wisdom in hindsight. It is very interesting that the author had kept a note of all those events and provided that as a compendium of instances with insights which will help any young entrepreneur in his journey. The firsthand narration of the events and the possible pitfalls and how those events could have been handled differently provides a greater insight to budding entrepreneurs. As Soren Kierkegaard said, "Life can only be understood backwards; but it must be lived forwards". This book is a good compilation of understanding the events in the author's professional career in a backward situation and provides solution in a practical way to handle things.

I think this book is a great initiative by the author with simple narration providing greater insight into various issues. I am sure that this book will make a good companion for any young entrepreneur in making their entrepreneurial journey both worthwhile and successful.

Venkatraman Balakrishnan

Former Chief Finance Officer [CFO], Infosys Limited

Co-Founder & Chairman, Exfinity Venture Partners

ACKNOWLEDGEMENTS

With 25+ years of top management experience I have worked across globe in a variety of industries. When I review the management failures I have lived through, I notice that a lot of people keep committing the same mistakes again and again. Management schools and programs give tips on how to succeed, but seldom gives warning on triggers of failure.

I thank my managers, peers and subordinates who have worked with me through the journey. For people who have even worked briefly with and under me, many of the experiences in this book will be relatable. There were times when I ignored saner advice and I am admitting them now through this book. When you are young and believe you exercise power, you have more proclivity to make mistakes.

I would like to sincerely thank my parents for giving me an upbringing that helps me stand back and acknowledge my own failures. That upbringing gives me the confidence to title this book — A Failure's Reminiscence. My wife scoffed and pleaded me not to label myself a failure. I however personally believe that failure is a steppingstone to success. If you have not failed enough times, you are either living within your comfort zone or not tried passionately enough to live your dream. I thank my wife, Rupa and children Varun and Pranati for standing by my side through this crazy journey

In my life journey, I have learnt a lot due to generosity of a few individuals. They have given me the freedom to sail and shared their time to help me analyze. I would like to list Mr. N Lakshman Rau, IAS Retd., Noted Karnataka Civil Servant; Dr. Krishna Murthy, Dr. SV Subramanuam, Dr. Vittal Rao and Dr. NS

A FAILURE'S REMINISCENCE
LESSONS FROM A LIFETIME OF MANAGEMENT BLUNDERS

Lakshman Rao – who guided me through my first entrepreneurial journey creating a science magazine for children; Kishan Ananthram and Brindala Ananthram – the promoters of IonIdea; Jim Wynn and Amrit Yegnanarayan – my colleagues at IonIdea and finally my wife, Rupa Rao, who invested her life savings in my current venture. She urged me to take a tough decision and move away from a comfortable job to reinitiate my entrepreneurial journey

I most sincerely thank one of India's finest financial managers and iconic CFO of Infosys and now a leading venture capitalist, Mr. V. Balakrishnan for his preface.

A FAILURE'S REMINISCENCE
LESSONS FROM A LIFETIME OF MANAGEMENT BLUNDERS

TABLE OF CONTENTS

Do Stock Options Promote Performance? 3
Reward Loyal Vendors 7
Long Tenures Isn't Loyalty 11
Incentivize Frontline Sales for Better Performance 15
Personal Risk Management – Manage brand equity ... 19
Strategy to Hire "Loyal" Employees 25
Don't Short-change Loyal Clients 28
Innovation – Hunting Ideas 32
Should Interviews Be Executive Priority? 35
Breaking Tasks – Key to Project Completion 40
Laser Focus Assures Success 44
Customer Selection – Sophistication = Growth 48
"Small Project Teams" Propel Success 52
Shaping Career - Employer Type Identification 56
Circle of Creativity 61
Psychological Market Leadership 66
Value Pricing Strategy 69
Should succession be a race? 73
Continuous success needs abandonment 77
Software career evolution – A perspective 81
Who Should Review Your Business Plans 85
Encourage employees to fire their boss 91
View your business as a customer 95
Have delivery teams face customers 99
Comprehensive contracts reduce risks 103
Business is about exploiting opportunities 107
Employee Selection – Focus on results 111
People are not cost 114

A FAILURE'S REMINISCENCE
LESSONS FROM A LIFETIME OF MANAGEMENT BLUNDERS

Endorsement pricing — A premium pricing strategy... 117
People Need Honest Feedback 120
Make Competition work for you 124
Communicate to motivate 128
Complete today's work — avoid email 132
The Challenge of reviews 136
Emotional aspect of support 140
Alternate business plans — reducing risk of closure ... 144
Expensive locations drive you out of business 148
Market Share and Profitability 152
What works in cost cutting 156
Executive freedom and customer excellence 160
Local Manufacturing — Success in foreign markets 164
Integrity & Business Practices 168
Founder Discord 172
Are Loyalty Schemes required? 176
Grading performances — does it make sense? 180
Phone policy reflects personal values 184
Operationalize integrity 189
Is Recruiting a HR function? 193
Should Exit Plan be Part of Business Plan? 196

A FAILURE'S REMINISCENCE
LESSONS FROM A LIFETIME OF MANAGEMENT BLUNDERS

Do Stock Options Promote Performance?

Stock options have been projected as one of the most important corporate compensation mechanism. The idea is that it helps align shareholder and executive interests and motivate the team to deliver on the same corporate goals.

The minimum expectation of every investor in a corporate activity is that the return on their investment beats inflation by eight to ten percent, if not more. If the returns are less, he would rather invest in index stocks or in bonds than to be an investor in a more risky venture.

Paying a percentage of cash to the person who contributes to its generation is a fair deal. It is the company's interest to share rewards, for so long as the person is active in its generation. Linking payoffs to profits rather than revenue is in company's long term interest.

Shares are a different kettle of fish. Anyone joining a start-up, putting their financial security and career at stake, and delivering continuous value, qualifies for a share in the company. That is what entrepreneurship is all about. However in a publicly traded organization with mature systems, the role of shares as a compensation tool is questionable.

A FAILURE'S REMINISCENCE
LESSONS FROM A LIFETIME OF MANAGEMENT BLUNDERS

One of the biggest traps, in a reward policy, in a traded organization, is to democratize the issue of shares to everyone in the organization. The thinking is that team work should be rewarded and the stocks can be a ruse to hold back an individual for a few years. Seldom do companies insist on achievement of performance standards over a period of time before the employee becomes eligible for shares. Endowing shares indiscriminately, at prices which are at a market discount, is actually rewarding mediocrity.

Most company policies enable shares to vest over a certain number of years. The thinking behind the principle is that employees understand that they have to deliver continuously to get a better deal for themselves. The reality is that company managements are sending a message that they are rewarding performance ahead of time. They are playing the role of punters, best left to the markets, rather than a delivery organization.

The subaltern message is that long tenures count and not actual performance. All people need to do to collect a bounty is stay and wait. Human nature being what it is, most of the people do just that. They expect their colleagues to deliver while they are content to collect their pay checks and team rewards and plan their retirement in company time. In most such cases, a small team has to push the envelope on behalf of everyone else.

A FAILURE'S REMINISCENCE
LESSONS FROM A LIFETIME OF MANAGEMENT BLUNDERS

Generous options make a larger subset of people wealthy. That is good. It also pushes away many people from delivering value. It is scary when mediocre people in early thirties contemplate retirement. It is not just a question of able people not contributing to the nation's wealth, but is more a talent drain.

Managing stocks are tricky enough. Huge swings in personal wealth unnerve people who do not understand the market. A choppy market makes the middle tier of the organization excessively focused on the market, rather than on their deadlines. The uncertainties and helplessness add to the stress levels. This is not in the organization's interest.

The worst part of the scenario is stocks bestowed on top management personnel. Many employment contracts stipulate that the person gets a certain number of shares as a retirement benefit, during exit. The incentive in these cases to deliver performance is very little. There is more incentive in such cases for the CXO to fail and be thrown out, rather than deliver value to the stakeholders. That is the worst nightmare for an investor.

LESSONS LEARNT
1. Link incentives to the bottom – line rather than top – line
2. Continued incentives must be linked to the actual contribution of the individual to the business / project

A FAILURE'S REMINISCENCE
LESSONS FROM A LIFETIME OF MANAGEMENT BLUNDERS

LESSONS LEARNT

3. Sharing wealth in a start – up through share allotment is justified. Giving shares to employees in a preferential mode in a traded organization is not warranted
4. If shares are issued in a running company, then set performance standards for realizing the shares. Tenure should not be the deciding criteria
5. Teach people how to manage their personal wealth. Their personal management of money has the key to your stable and efficient delivery operations
6. While deciding stock options for executive management teams, don't build a contract that makes it personally rewarding for a CxO to be thrown out of a job rather than stay and fight

A FAILURE'S REMINISCENCE
LESSONS FROM A LIFETIME OF MANAGEMENT BLUNDERS

Reward Loyal Vendors

All of us associate loyalty programs with customers. Companies encourage clients stay and spend. It is also a standard practice to recognize long serving employees. Seldom do companies believe that loyal vendors deserve similar recognition.

Some of my clients tell me that their patronage is a gift that we should thankful about. A few others communicate that they pay only their best vendors on time. I know of companies that insist their vendors to borrow money from their finance subsidiaries, in case your payment gets struck with them and you insist that they pay. In many parts of the world, business people take this attitude as being on par.

It is however equally true is that the companies that respect vendors are also the most successful.

If there is a management recognition that vendors invest in our business and are to be treated in the same manner that an investor is to be treated, the relationship assumes greater maturity.

Good vendors bring tremendous value to business. The value goes beyond the size of the order and most times are extremely strategic to business. Good vendors are difficult to get. The best vendors prefer to work with stable and large organizations that

A FAILURE'S REMINISCENCE
LESSONS FROM A LIFETIME OF MANAGEMENT BLUNDERS

pay on time. Vendors also categorize clients and account managers prefer to support clients who can help them meet their sales and revenue targets.

Categorizing vendors, based on the value they deliver and their relative investments to our business, is a simple way to gain loyalty. When vendors are made to feel special, they normally tend to prioritize our requirements.

Helping vendors meet their revenue targets, when they deliver superior value, is another manner of vendor recognition. This can be achieved either by increasing the order size or by actively promoting the company among other suppliers, who can use their services. I have personally felt the pressure of higher expectations, every time a client recommends us to another person.

In the corporate world, client entertainment is an everyday affair. Great companies are also known to entertain and reward vendors. Public recognition for good work done motivates managements to assign more bandwidth and deliver higher value to the particular client.

One of the best ways to bridge trust deficits with vendors is by being more transparent and integrating them into the strategic framework. Trusted vendors can be involved right from inception stage of the project. They can be motivated to contribute their technical mite in product design. Using their competencies and technical expertise during the initial design stages can help us identify feasible design alternatives and reduce cost substantially. Delivery plans can be implemented most realistically without building scope creep into the project.

I have contributed many times for my clients to win business. Companies form consortiums to win deals by just showcasing collective competencies. In most of such collaborations, the smaller partners bring more value to the table than the principal player. Trust and sharing are what makes the other party contribute and invest in our success. Transparency and effectiveness also implies sharing a percentage of the benefits with the vendor teams.

Clients can also show appreciation for the relationship, by providing technical and infrastructural support to vendors. It may not cost much money to have a small team guide vendors in a strategic manner that will help them reduce costs and increase margins. Senior and experienced shop floor workers can even contribute as mentors in this task. There is a tremendous spill-off, from a loyalty perspective, when we help smaller companies improve their core competency and ability to deliver.

Any action that goes beyond patronage and helps the other party succeed is what demonstrates a mature relationship. Maturity

A FAILURE'S REMINISCENCE
LESSONS FROM A LIFETIME OF MANAGEMENT BLUNDERS

breeds loyalty and helps deliver better deal to the investors and employees.

This is not to suggest that we stop negotiating the best deals for our organizations. All the above steps are true, only when the vendor demonstrates ability to deliver quality consistently and brings value to our process and the client.

LESSONS LEARNT

1. Good vendors are difficult to get. The best companies choose their clients
2. Recognize that vendors are investing in our business
3. Help good vendors meet their revenue targets – give them a higher share of your business and recommend them to others. They reciprocate with trust and better deliveries
4. Entertain and reward good vendors
5. Involve vendors during design – they know more about their products / industry than you do

A FAILURE'S REMINISCENCE
LESSONS FROM A LIFETIME OF MANAGEMENT BLUNDERS

Long Tenures Isn't Loyalty

"Employee Retention" is one of the key factors on which an organization's HR Policy is evaluated. Most successful organizations also have a strong mid-tier level with a long track record within the organization. They provide the skeleton around which companies plan growth and managements commit deliveries.

That raises the key question – are organizations doing the right thing by equating longevity with loyalty?

People continue to stay in an organization for a wide variety of reasons. Most people look for stability, even while they would like to see growth in their careers. As long as they see the organization providing career satisfaction and work – life stability, they stick to the company. Companies, and indeed individual managers, have a responsibility to help the person grow professionally and financially.

Loyalty is unfortunately a two way street. Much as employees would like to see growth, they have a sacred duty to contribute to the companies and to its core objectives. Each one of us has a responsibility to bring value to our client – both internal to the company and a paying customer.

All persons come with a cost. The cost is not just salary and benefits. It also includes

A FAILURE'S REMINISCENCE
LESSONS FROM A LIFETIME OF MANAGEMENT BLUNDERS

infrastructure costs, administration costs and opportunity cost. A thumb rule is that these costs are a minimum of two times your actual cost to company. You break even when you meet these costs and contribute when your direct revenue, post taxes, are greater than the costs. As a manager, your costs include the costs of all persons who report to you directly and indirectly. As long as you contribute to your company, you are an asset to the organization. Otherwise, you are a liability.

With every increment to our pay and perks, we carry a greater expectation from the client. We need to deliver higher value to the client to justify the increased cost. If the value increases with experience, then there is a justification in demanding higher salaries and reimbursement. Otherwise, we start adding to costs and become a liability to the organization. All clients have a right, and a responsibility to their stakeholders, to evaluate value for the services they pay for and move towards any organization that gives them better value. The key issue is the value that costs bring – not costs by themselves.

Successful companies define and quantify the value each employee brings to the client. They clearly define the successful outcome and train their employees to achieve the outcome every single time, by reducing risks that contribute to employee's failure.

A FAILURE'S REMINISCENCE
LESSONS FROM A LIFETIME OF MANAGEMENT BLUNDERS

Successful organizations build a compensation structure that has a low base, but a strong incentive for the employee to complete the desired outcome over and over. The overall package is attractive for a performer to stay and contribute. These organizations actually build the self-esteem of the employee with each pay slip.

Organizations that rewards tenure tends to attract a crowd that believes that they have a right to a cozy lifestyle for just showing up. In most of these organizations, promotions mean less work and more time for meetings and manoeuvres. Hierarchy does not mean more responsibility, but more perks.

You can recognize these organizations by their extremely good pay structure. The well-endowed benefits structure is linked to the hierarchy. Most of these companies talk about equality and tend to place an upper limit to incentives or better still have an incentives budget.

These wonderful organizations are great places for the lazy and the lowly to spend time waiting for retirement. These organizations always attract good people, who join to learn and run – somebody has to generate revenue anyway. You would find the most number of loyal employees in such a vile environment.

A FAILURE'S REMINISCENCE
LESSONS FROM A LIFETIME OF MANAGEMENT BLUNDERS

LESSONS LEARNT

1. Key issue is the value that costs bring – not the costs by themselves
2. If you're direct and indirect costs do not increase in value, you become a cost to the organization. Your clients have a responsibility to evaluate your need in their scheme of things
3. Build a compensation structure with a reasonable base and an incentive scheme that rewards meeting client objectives consistently

A FAILURE'S REMINISCENCE
LESSONS FROM A LIFETIME OF MANAGEMENT BLUNDERS

Incentivize Frontline Sales for Better Performance

Sales incentives are tricky business. Incentives have proved to be the most effective method to incentivize an otherwise good sales person to deliver. They assure good returns for effort spent and help to increase self-worth of the individual with every pay check.

In most organizations, the HR policy focuses on the same salary structure for the entire sales organization. The ratio of base to incentives is same across board. In most cases, it is the operations management that decides the incentive plan. Since the base increases across the sales hierarchy, the operation sales management structures the incentive scheme to reflect the incentive distribution in the same ratio.

The top management, not directly client facing gets up to 70% of the total incentive disbursed, while the frontline sales team gets around 25% to 30%. The best case scenario is generally 60% - 40%. This structure is normally accepted since the operating principal apparently is linked to the existing minimum revenue base and a maximum commission cap that employment contracts carry.

The frontline sales team normally defines the client experience. Clients associate their brand exposure to just their experience with

A FAILURE'S REMINISCENCE
LESSONS FROM A LIFETIME OF MANAGEMENT BLUNDERS

frontline personnel. Seldom do clients sit back and analyse the investments managements make in infrastructure and policies, if their experience with the sales or customer support executive sucks. People tend to switch brands, not because your IT Infrastructure sucks or the canteen in your HQ is not better equipped, but because, the front line executive brings frustration to the experience. The one big difference managements can make to their revenues and the brand is by increasing the effectiveness of this interface.

Companies that regard and reward their frontline sales team also tend to give them more flexibility and decision making authorities to deliver. Building a mature partnership structure will possibly boost sales more than any other initiative you can plan.

What constitutes the mature partnership? The relationship is built on four significant pillars.

The first and most important function is to attract and select the right person for the job. This is extremely basic, but seldom done. When someone is not committed to a career in customer facing role and does not enjoy people interface, the result shows. Just walk into any mall, or franchisee based sales / customer support organization, and you experience it all the time. Having such people on any kind of incentive structure is a

A FAILURE'S REMINISCENCE
LESSONS FROM A LIFETIME OF MANAGEMENT BLUNDERS

waste of time, since these people seldom qualify for the incentive and their frustration translates into customer dejection.

Continuous technical training and individual skill enhancement programs are extremely crucial for continuous success. Customer evaluation keeps evolving with the alternate information channels available to them. They expect the professional to be better informed about the industry, products and features. It is not fair for the organization to expect their sales staff to handle clients on the basis of their native intelligence always. Dumb dolls do not necessarily translate to business. Sharing experiences often is an effective training mode.

Evolving a team structure that respects the individual is another key. Huge discrepancies between managers and field staff; pro-active information sharing; transparency in commercial transactions internally; recognition of success; and most importantly the basis of incentive sharing are some of the areas where this team matrix comes under focus. It helps if senior management do not delegate indiscriminately in these areas.

Sharing a larger part of the incentive with the field staff makes a large difference. It helps to build a transparent structure and explain their basis to the team. The team must realize that the managements are committed to give them a fair share of profits

A FAILURE'S REMINISCENCE
LESSONS FROM A LIFETIME OF MANAGEMENT BLUNDERS

from the business they help generate. It is even more important that the incentives are paid on time and without reminders.

Companies may want to look at a different HR structure for their sales managers and field staff. However the act of enabling field staff to make more money rests with the managers and the organization.

Fixing your field staff organization brings faster rewards and enduring customer loyalty.

LESSONS LEARNT

1. Choose people who enjoy client interface in sales positions
2. The proportion of base: incentive, as a percentage, must be in inverse proportion to their hierarchy. Those people facing the customer must earn a higher percentage of incentive than those sitting in head office.
3. Allow frontline sales persons to exercise more operational freedom
4. Customers have access to multiple tools to educate themselves. Your sales persons must keep up the knowledge spiral by continuously updating themselves

A FAILURE'S REMINISCENCE
LESSONS FROM A LIFETIME OF MANAGEMENT BLUNDERS

Personal Risk Management – Manage brand equity

Risk management is an area where project managers have strong opinions. There are two aspects to risk management – "project risks" and "personal risks". Project managers instinctively identify and address project risks.

Personal risks are those that affect the credibility and stature of the project manager. These have nothing to do with the project, but relate more to how the manager is able to communicate the cause and effect of risks to clients, teams and the management. These are seldom understood and even less appreciated by project managers.

How much information should one share is a tricky question. I have seen project managers not communicate important situations to their top management and clients, either because they believe they can manage the situation independently; or because they have no mitigation plans to propose; or simply because they believe that the problem can't be resolved within the organization; or sometimes, because they lose face. Not losing face is a cultural issue.

On the other hand, I have heard project managers say that they listed 5,000 risks, just because the size of the project is $1 million. The entire list is shared with

A FAILURE'S REMINISCENCE
LESSONS FROM A LIFETIME OF MANAGEMENT BLUNDERS

everyone concerned [client included]. If left at that, it stops at being an academic exercise.

My experience of dealing with clients on software projects regarding risk sharing has been tricky. Some clients see the risk list and comment that they may have made a mistake in giving us their project – a long risk list is perceived as a "failure – in – the – making". On the other hand, I have come across clients, who are happy that we have listed so many risks and have a mitigation plan ahead of time. The client participation ends with that. Only an intelligent assessment of customer SPOC execution maturity can determine how risks should be presented in review meetings and client discussions. Risks Mitigation Plans have to tailored, according to our perception, of the audience.

The related issue concerns client / management related risks. Seldom does a project review exclusively focus on customers' (/ managements') contribution to the risk and what the client manager has done to eliminate client related risks. If brought up aggressively in meetings, it is seen as building excuses for later failure. If downplayed, the risks actually materialize and assure project failure. I have deployed two strategies successfully to manage this crucial aspect.

The first is to use the email as a tool to repeatedly highlight each and every risk and

A FAILURE'S REMINISCENCE
LESSONS FROM A LIFETIME OF MANAGEMENT BLUNDERS

suggest practical measures for their mitigation with time frames. The solution can be a meeting with all concerned stakeholders' or sending alternate budget proposals, so decisions can be made. Even if procurement does not come under our purview, if we can suggest alternatives, the general management tendency is to hold you accountable for results. The risks of failure are eliminated to a large extent if you are in the loop on decision making and implementation.

The other alternative is to schedule meeting with specific stakeholders' with the concerned topics only on agenda. If the person is a senior officer or a client, the ruse is to request for ideas for mitigation. The minutes should hopefully include action items to reduce or eliminate the risk.

One other best practice that key stakeholders' appreciate is, if the manager presents the risks and danger he foresees to the project, during the next review period. A project sponsor would always like to know that something may not happen as per plan well in advance. This is a responsibility that many managers forget.

I have never come across a review where the management appreciates the mitigation implemented by a project manager, if there is no mention of the risk occurrence and its mitigation. I have actually led projects, and been on review mode, my entire lifetime. My experience suggests that the manager should speak about the risk occurrence and mitigation attempted, very briefly, during reviews. As long as the attempt is neither to brag nor to put down others, reviewers get comfort that the project is in safe hands.

It is important to update the mitigation plan each week and explain the reasons why new risks are perceived in the project in review meetings. This approach will assure all stakeholders that the manager has control of the project. It will help him save jobs, since failure can seldom be held against the manager or his core team in such a situation.

The key thing is not how many risks were listed or mitigation proposed, but how many really critical risks are tracked and how quickly these are escalated. There is no bravado in holding back critical information.

The mantra is essentially to share the bad news at the earliest. Let them know the bad news from you, rather than from outsiders. The emphasis of status reporting is to be on key drivers which affect the fulfilment of project objectives and risks which are beyond the scope of the project team. These are important secrets to manage "personal" risks with project sponsors and key management personnel.

It is always a good habit to list risks from a systemic view point. Risks at project inception vary widely with those at project

A FAILURE'S REMINISCENCE
LESSONS FROM A LIFETIME OF MANAGEMENT BLUNDERS

transition. Most interdependencies can be reasonably listed during project planning. Involvement of peers and support departments at that stage and taking their inputs in planning helps reduce frustrations and heartburn.

To help colleagues not let one down, it is best practice to call them into discussions and meetings and ask them to review parts of your plans that concern them and their deliverable. Any critical input that in your opinion can risk the project must be addressed ahead of time taking the support teams into confidence. Taking up an issue jointly at the beginning of the project helps top management plan resource allocation.

Involving peers in project plan reviews and helping them plan their deliverables / resources ahead of time builds critical personal brand equity within the company.

The challenges within the team are a different challenge. With many techies, technology for its own sake becomes more important than the objectives in a development team. Staffing risks can be identified through close interaction with the team. Having team risk meetings is a good strategy to identify development, estimation, architectural and design risks and plug them early. Teams participate actively in risk identification and contribute in mitigation if the project manager respects the team and is transparent about the whole process.

A FAILURE'S REMINISCENCE
LESSONS FROM A LIFETIME OF MANAGEMENT BLUNDERS

As one moves up the hierarchy, there is sometimes an erroneous belief that information should be shared on a need basis. The ability to deliver comes from capacity to trust other stakeholders and make it easier for them to do their jobs.

LESSONS LEARNT
1. Project managers must consider risk management not just from project perspective, but also from their personal growth perspective
2. Let everyone concerned know about the risks that concern them ahead of time
3. Let them know the bad news from you rather than from an outsider
4. It is not sufficient to manage risks, but also let everyone know what risks have occurred and what mitigation strategy worked

A FAILURE'S REMINISCENCE
LESSONS FROM A LIFETIME OF MANAGEMENT BLUNDERS

Strategy to Hire "Loyal" Employees

For people of my generation, in India, who have seen job transition from public sector and banks to new generation industries, frequent job changes seem a strange phenomenon. I often meet and speak to people who spent their entire lives in but a few organizations. They are happy ambassadors of their companies.

What makes people stay and contribute to companies? What kind of talent grows to become a company's iron frame? How can we create an environment to bring more such people through the door?

Alignment of a recruit to company values is extremely important. When a person identifies his personality with the company, it becomes very difficult for him to move out of the comfort zone. Lifelong employments in companies like TATA, Birla, Reliance, Infosys, TVS and WIPRO are not uncommon. In most of these organizations, employees find others very much like themselves in thinking and outlook. If a person does not find a need to quit in the first three years, you can be reasonably sure that he will contribute for a sufficient long time in the company. It is imperative for interviewers along the value chain to ask questions and explain the company value system. Most candidates opt out when they realize that their value system

A FAILURE'S REMINISCENCE
LESSONS FROM A LIFETIME OF MANAGEMENT BLUNDERS

and character traits do not gel with the company.

Larger, visible and profitable companies appear stable. They meet the security and social needs of a person. Persons from secure background [children of employees in government, banks, public sector and other large corporate] and those with family responsibilities look for employment in large organizations and stable jobs. In sectors like the Information Technology, there is an option of moving between tier I companies within the same city. Not every one in every industry and location has similar advantages. It is not just sufficient to manage a company well. It is equally important to let the world know that you are running stable operations.

Hiring known people generally guarantees more stable workforce. However, it is not a bad idea to interface and interact with the family of the employees, at the time of recruitment. This is especially important when you hire young professionals, freshmen or young people moving to a new city. These interviews reveal a lot about the circumstances and behaviour pattern of the candidate. Even more importantly, the family members become a part of the mutually supportive environment for the young person. Family association is a strong and invisible counter against peer pressures that an immature person encounters at worksite.

A FAILURE'S REMINISCENCE
LESSONS FROM A LIFETIME OF MANAGEMENT BLUNDERS

Coming from the service industry, I understand the concept of hiring just-in-time and avoiding bench. A focused service offering always gives us flexibility to manage with a bench for short period of time. Rank opportunism in attracting business or not bothering to build a core competency in the name of entrepreneurship or dynamism, is immaturity. Immature companies and managements attract equally opportunistic workforce. The way managements react to surges and troughs give strong signals to employees and they react to these signals in a manner that they believe is in their self-interest. It is no wonder that companies with large scale iteration are also companies with least specialization and that includes a vast majority of companies in the information technology, ITES and retail sector.

Loyal employees are a result of a mature recruitment strategy. It is never an accident. If you want your liquid assets to stay put, it is imperative to bring in the right capital in the first place. The alternative is to becoming a paid training centre to your competitor.

LESSONS LEARNT
1. Focus on personal values
2. Let the World know that you are managing your company well
3. Focus on core competency while picking orders – train people

A FAILURE'S REMINISCENCE
LESSONS FROM A LIFETIME OF MANAGEMENT BLUNDERS

Don't Short-change Loyal Clients

Four generations in our family have been reading the same newspaper for over seven decades. It is the costliest newspaper in the country and we continue the tradition. Some time back, an employee of the newspaper knocked on the door, in the name of conducting a survey. We gave him details that he asked for. At the end, he said that the real reason for the survey was to offer the newspaper to newer subscribers at 20% of the existing cost. Since we read the newspaper for decades, we were not eligible for the scheme.

It is quite understandable that the newspaper wants to enlarge its client base. The plan and execution however was built in a manner that advertised loud and clear to its existing patrons that it was rewarding trust with abuse. The message I understood from the transaction was that the newspaper was taking its patrons for granted. It was prepared to reward new customers rather than loyal ones. I changed the newspaper subscription in the presence of the company personnel. He was aghast. I requested him to come home during his next visit and I would oblige him with a subscription. He was extremely happy to lose an existing customer [and our billing] for a period, since we helped him meet his numbers by coming in as a new customer.

A FAILURE'S REMINISCENCE
LESSONS FROM A LIFETIME OF MANAGEMENT BLUNDERS

From my perspective, it was a total loss to the newspaper organization. The management lost my trust about its ability to be fair. It paid a salary to its sales representative to help me defect to a competitor and lose revenue for his company. It again incentivized him to get me back into the system losing 80% revenue on a daily basis for a full year. I am sure that the organization would be paying the sales head a fat bonus for this stupidity.

Getting newer clients is an expensive affair. Managements most times are like Napoleon. They spill blood to conquer more territories and continuously demonstrate their prowess to capture new markets. The blood spill after all is a waste, since the King seldom demonstrates his hold on the territory even for a short time and is able to justify the hard work through sustained revenues.

Mature clients standardize on their growth partners early in all aspects of their business. They reduce their risks of delivery through a dual system of building processes and by working with known companies. When companies give stable business to their vendors, they expect the vendors to return the compliment, in kind, by providing excellent support at lower prices. It is the duty of the vendor to enable their clients to win.

When newer customers get better value or rates or both for the same service, you are

A FAILURE'S REMINISCENCE
LESSONS FROM A LIFETIME OF MANAGEMENT BLUNDERS

advertising loudly that you no longer value business from your older customers. You encourage them to look beyond you and defect. When clients understand that you have taken them for granted, they talk with their feet.

Sales organizations and many B2B clients believe it is a fair deal to offer the same service to different clients at different prices. Culturally we would like to bargain continuously on every aspect of the deal. People are aghast when they are confronted by a notice that discourages negotiation. Giving differential prices to people who know and can demand better deals leaves the other person frustrated. One of the reasons why people unconsciously move to organized retailers is because the system treats every one equally. This is a message most managements forget.

While growth should be constant, we need to understand the real cost of expansion. It helps to put in place a system to calculate the actual costs of customer retention, customer acquisition and customer defection. Managements may be surprised that their growth targets are easier met by lower cost, account management teams rather than high profile, business development teams.

It is always profitable to put our client's best interests above our sales and revenue targets, if we want to see long term growth and profits.

A FAILURE'S REMINISCENCE
LESSONS FROM A LIFETIME OF MANAGEMENT BLUNDERS

LESSONS LEARNT

1. When you offer better terms to newer customers, when compared to existing customers, you advertise loudly that you don't value existing business
2. Customers move to organized retailers in search of fairer terms is a strong message to all sellers that it pays to be fair in their dealings with their clients
3. Understand the real cost of expansion, before you embark on client acquisition

A FAILURE'S REMINISCENCE
LESSONS FROM A LIFETIME OF MANAGEMENT BLUNDERS

Innovation – Hunting Ideas

"Innovation" & "Best Practices" are among the management jargons that top executives seem to love. No presentation is complete without the liberal usage of these jargons.

Innovation is a desired feature of every living organization. The barometer for innovation is patents. That is one of the obvious ways to capitalize an intellectual property and legally manage technological advances introduced within the company. From a patent perspective it does not appear that many organizations practice innovation. Big names with large turnover normally have extremely few patents to their credit.

This does not mean that organizations do not have intelligent people who create. There were so many best practices that my teams followed, but were never documented anywhere and appreciated, much less formally patented. We created innovative solutions that were later patented by larger product companies, when our team members joined them. We lost the claim to the innovation since I was never able to put together a comprehensive return of investment justification for spending our time and money to patent all those innovations that we did on projects.

Companies can actually make innovation happen just by focusing on idea creation. They do not necessarily have to spend

A FAILURE'S REMINISCENCE
LESSONS FROM A LIFETIME OF MANAGEMENT BLUNDERS

millions on R&D teams to create an intellectual property. My own belief is that they must be necessarily be business driven and must be customer led. Most innovation I am involved has happened when we were under extreme [and unreasonable] customer pressure to deliver quality and results.

Companies can't bank on genius to deliver innovation. Hiring extremely great talent is not an option for most organizations. The best people to do innovation are those who know the process well and are open to ideas. When people on the firing line are given a realizable & purposeful target, they think through solutions that will help them manage the problem better.

The term "open to ideas" means that the person must have the habit of listening. They must be open to suggestions and have experiences that are dissimilar to us and have a new perspective. I constantly receive ideas during casual conversations and coffee shop talk. Listening to decision makers shares their pain points and / or experiences or negating your ideas are other situations where many intelligent possibilities emerge. When we assimilate different ideas & thoughts from different sources and map them to our own business experience, myriad intellectual assets are possibilities.

Any idea that does not help improve either the customer experience or profitability or both is not really worth spending time on.

A FAILURE'S REMINISCENCE
LESSONS FROM A LIFETIME OF MANAGEMENT BLUNDERS

When ideas can be monetized and persons incentivized, then the ecology to seed innovation happens automatically.

There are enough instances where R&D happens in isolation. R&D in many companies [and even defence] is the CEO's holy cow. If business does not drive R&D, innovation normally becomes expensive. I know of innovative companies where the R&D reports to the marketing teams and works closely with them to help clients become successful.

If companies encourage everyone along the line to focus on specific cost based or function - enhancement projects, innovation happens seamlessly. The culture to file patents and demonstrate monetary aspect of innovation in internal and external reports is something that will then become a powerful habit.

LESSONS LEARNT

1. Focus on those small innovations that your project teams bring to the table
2. Innovation requires an open mind and complete understanding of the process. When people are pushed to try alternatives, then innovation happens by itself
3. People must be open to listen to dis-similar experiences
4. Allow business to drive innovation – innovation in isolation is generally expensive and tends to become holy cows

A FAILURE'S REMINISCENCE
LESSONS FROM A LIFETIME OF MANAGEMENT BLUNDERS

Should Interviews Be Executive Priority?

Interviews are the last things talented technocrats want to do. Everyone suddenly becomes very busy when you suggest they take up interviews. Deadlines seem to suddenly become extremely sacrosanct or people have to visit hometowns for their grandma's funeral that weekend.

That leaves talent acquisition teams and project managers identify those persons who normally do not contribute much to the team to take up interviews.

Having poor contributors take interviews leads to two serious consequences. They lower the overall technical standard of interviews and also keep away extremely good candidates from getting selected since they view them as threats.

One thing common about poor contributors across organizations is their morale. They are either "poor selections" who can't perform in their role or who have been "kicked upstairs" with no ability to deliver or worse still those people who are in it only for money and can't learn or enjoy their job.

Smart candidates assess the interviewer's ability much faster than the interviewer short listing the consultant. The attitude, interviews' focus [or lack of it], technical depth and the body language reveals a lot of things about the current mental status of the interviewer. Good candidates are generally unwilling to join organizations where their bosses can't also be competent mentors and show themselves as incapable.

Organizations must make talent selection a badge of honour, rather than an unwelcome chore. The company's best resources must seriously contribute effectively if you want to sell the company and the job to a potential employee. An hour's investment to select the right person will mean a lot less effort to make deliveries happen every day.

Having top management involved keenly in selection process normally makes interview a more serious affair. Across the hierarchy, the executive management must emphasize the importance of bringing in the right talent with appropriate background into the team.

It is necessary for delivery managers to work closely with the talent acquisition teams to identify the best [and the busiest] young stars to be a part of the interview panel. Making membership of the interview panel a pre-requisite for promotion normally attracts the cream and the ambitious to contribute strongly to the process.

It is not difficult to estimate time for each interview and encourage people to budget the time as a part of their weekly deliverables. Delivery managers must make it a point to let the team know that only the best

A FAILURE'S REMINISCENCE
LESSONS FROM A LIFETIME OF MANAGEMENT BLUNDERS

performers will be given the honour of conducting interviews.

A short meeting of the panel across hierarchies can decide the scope of interviews at each stage [basically the parameters for rejection, rather than selection]. This gives the best and brightest an opportunity to interface with seniors in the organization and aspire for higher reaches. It is also a powerful motivational aspect for other team members to be a part of the interview panel. Offering non-monetary recognition for people who take time off after office hours, on weekends and holidays to conduct interviews is another best practice that helps retain enthusiasm to conduct interviews when candidates are free. Lunch coupons; holiday packages; pizzas and pasta treats; theatre or movie tickets with family; team lunch for the entire panel; are some of the suggested alternatives to let the employee and his family know that their effort is appreciated.

End of the day, the difference between paying a premium for a dud and identifying the right person for every slot is a conscious management decision. Smart managers plan their hires, clarify the exact role of each member and place a price for being a team member.

There is one caution about bringing mid – level and junior managers into the interview cycle. Their personal immaturity or tendency

A FAILURE'S REMINISCENCE
LESSONS FROM A LIFETIME OF MANAGEMENT BLUNDERS

to display knowledge or highlight relative ignorance about a subject puts off candidates. This situation is best managed by pairing interviewers with a HR representative.

The other issue I have noticed when mid – level professionals are brought in to the interview cycle is rejection of talented persons based on salary. An innocuous question about the current salary and expected salary is always answered in affirmative. Interviewers reject the candidate saying that he is not worth the salary he is seeking. The interviewer himself may not be drawing the salary the candidate is seeking. It may even be a convenient reason to mask any other personal reason for rejection.

At the other extreme, many managers believe that the entry into their teams is like membership into an exclusive club. They encourage team members to look for reasons to reject candidates and display their badge of exclusivity proudly. This kills the company in long run.

LESSONS LEARNT
1. Get your best people to interview
2. Start with a process to reject and not select
3. Don't pick your worst team members to be on interview panel
4. Let interviews not be a platform to test relative knowledge
5. Pair a HR person with mid – level technical persons in interviews

6. Decision on salaries must happen initially when HR takes a decision to invite the candidate for an interview or at the time of selection where a decision maker makes the call – it should not be a factor at every stage of selection

A FAILURE'S REMINISCENCE
LESSONS FROM A LIFETIME OF MANAGEMENT BLUNDERS

Breaking Tasks – Key to Project Completion

One of the biggest hurdles in project completion is the assumed size of the task. Most projects never get started since it looks too daunting. When project looks unlikely to complete, procrastination steps in. We are never sure where to begin.

The most effective way to manage a project [whether individual or organizational] is to understand the scope of deliverables first. It is always necessary to begin with the end in mind. Once there is clarity in destination, the alternate routes identify by themselves. Consultants, with varied experiences and core competency, can add perspectives to identify these alternatives.

Identifying potential execution risks are vital to finalizing on an execution approach. Experience and expertise are the wisest counsel in this area. In their absence, listing areas where there is no clarity is a good approach. Once the risks are known, even the most difficult tasks suddenly become easy to execute.

However for projects to complete, it is necessary to break down each task as finitely as possible. The key to such a definition is always to quantify the deliverable. It could be as mundane as a sales target in case of a sales project, number of hires in the case of a recruitment project, marks for a student or

A FAILURE'S REMINISCENCE
LESSONS FROM A LIFETIME OF MANAGEMENT BLUNDERS

numbers based acceptance plan in the case of a software project. My own belief is that if the team can't drive down to a quantitative definition, then they have not defined the solution adequately. The danger of defining the destination as we go along ceases. Waste and rework is eliminated in the process.

Once the deliverable is clear, it is always necessary to identify alternate routes and understand the risks of each alternative. Planning becomes critical. Every person plans – the key difference is the detail. Planning can be done at different stages and at different depths. Deeper the insight; better would be appreciation of risks & problems and higher possibility of success. "Divide and conquer" is the logic behind this simple, but effective management advice.

While every manager agrees on this aspect of practice, the greatest difficulty is the actual method of such work breakdown. In software projects, we divide the projects based on functionality, managers, objects or / and methods within each function. There are other fancy technical descriptions like "top-down" method and "bottom-up" method etc.

However, the real function of breakdown comes from identifying successive deliverables and the conditions [or dependencies] to meet each deliverables. A deliverable itself becomes a project in the new setting, and the challenge is to identify smaller deliverables and the conditions to meet such deliverables. The more sub-projects we identify, the better are our chances of success.

We know that we are on right track, if each activity can be completed in a few hours. The manager should be able to say with certainty that the activity is 100% complete. We have identified the right persons to execute the task, and they have reasonable clarity on how to approach and complete the task. Most importantly, everyone in the group knows when to raise his hands and indicate to all stakeholders if he has not completed his task.

The question most of us ask – "Is there value to such linear planning"? The answer to this question reveals the cultural experiences of the person and every point of view is right and relevant. What is not debatable is that failures are far and fewer when you plan and deliver rather than otherwise.

The next question about planning pertains to the challenges one should focus in the earliest stages of project execution. Some people believe that it is better to attack the tougher challenges and critical risks first and then complete the relatively easy tasks later. My own belief is that it is better to put most of the easier tasks [certainly, all those that the team can own and deliver in a heartbeat] in the first set of deliverables and use the intermediate time to plan and execute those work breakdowns that need research and

A FAILURE'S REMINISCENCE
LESSONS FROM A LIFETIME OF MANAGEMENT BLUNDERS

external help. Whatever the approach, it is true that all tasks must be completed for the project to get completed.

Does all this planning need a trained professional to execute? I personally don't think so. It is more about how we train our brain and the habits we pick up that matter more than the tool or the logic behind the plan. If you learn to break your work day into chunks of 90 or 120 minutes; work by an alarm and start each task as soon as the alarm sounds; eliminate all distractions [including phone and email]; and focus on completing the work you set out for the period, you will see that you have more time on your hands than you ever thought.

LESSONS LEARNT

1. Breakdown each task as finitely as possible – the best planned activity must not take more than a few hours
2. Keep a clear deliverable at the end of each cycle – define the deliverable quantitatively
3. Let each deliverable become an independent project
4. Keep in mind the dependencies for the succeeding activity, when you define the deliverable

A FAILURE'S REMINISCENCE
LESSONS FROM A LIFETIME OF MANAGEMENT BLUNDERS

Laser Focus Assures Success

In old movies, a rich man was shown to own a conglomerate. The display board before the office indicated ownership of every kind of business from finance to trading to manufacturing and agriculture.

In a license regime, you could not grow your business beyond a stage. Growth necessarily spread in whichever directions you were allowed to grow. Old time groups like TATAs and Birla are present in a large number of industries, with very little specialization and sparing core competencies.

Early stage software companies like TCS, Infosys and Wipro got opportunities to spread wings across technologies. As long the value proposition remained lower cost and bigger bandwidth, technology competency did not matter. They were providing bodies, onsite and offshore, with software capabilities.

Over time, restructuring happened. Many groups and companies are working on creating global scale in a few areas. They are letting go operations that does not contribute to the global vision and building core competencies in areas which will help them build value and scale in their chosen area.

This lesson however is not so apparent to dynamic entrepreneurs with risk taking capabilities. Many organizations would like to

A FAILURE'S REMINISCENCE
LESSONS FROM A LIFETIME OF MANAGEMENT BLUNDERS

take on all work that comes their way. Managements see that as a way forward for survival and to keep the cash flow going. While it may seem to be a practical way to move ahead, they sadly lose twin advantages – time and capital.

In today's situation, organizations need to have a clear vision to continuously provide the best market value to the client. We need to constantly innovate to provide more at lesser prices; investors have more choices and failures are accompanied by large risks for all stakeholders.

Managements today have challenges to ensure that their leadership time is invested in deepening relationships with their best customers and partners who help propel your vision. It is a good idea to define the key result areas for each business function and to set a target to the executive team to reach or exceed the KRA. The KRA may or may not be linked to sales and profits [which is important], but must necessarily be linked to achieve strategic edge to the organization. When leadership team runs with a clear focus, it aids the company get leadership position that guarantees future success and steady cash flow.

The frontline leadership and delivery command need to only focus on delivering client commitments consistently. They bring in cash flow. Any change in their focus will invite disaster. Line managers must best invest their time to reduce delivery risks and improve organizational performance by increasing process stability and scalability. Priority for capital and marketing investments become very clear and non-controversial, when strategic and tactical goals are very clear to everyone within the organization.

All investment proposals can be very clearly benchmarked to meet factors that hold us from becoming the best in the area. Each investment must help increase customer value. Vague and unproductive proposals drop, when proposers are asked to evaluate and define investment perspective from customer value standpoint.

Clear focus helps us in another manner. People who identify with the vision and can help us reach the goals stick with the organization. People who can't relate to the goals or the vision also leave the organization. The less the chances of excuses, less likely useless folks stay back.

To succeed and deliver long term, managements should focus all its time, efforts and resources to be the world's best in a small, but significant area. That is the best insurance against all external threats and unstable work environments.

LESSONS LEARNT

1. Define your business as clearly as possible. The KRA must be known to everyone
2. All investments [capital, time, opportunities] should be relative to the achievement of the objectives
3. Don't pick up any business that is thrown your way – pick opportunities that can help you reach your goal

A FAILURE'S REMINISCENCE
LESSONS FROM A LIFETIME OF MANAGEMENT BLUNDERS

Customer Selection – Sophistication = Growth

In an era, where growth is GOD, and stakeholders like large and instant appreciation to their personal capital, selective customer acquisition may seem like a strange concept. It can even be heresy to business heads.

All organizations, however large, can deliver the best market value to a specific class of clients. Their delivery management, process and cash flow are suitable for handling certain classes of customers. Identification of customers, to whom we can add larger value, is a key management task.

Client acquisition is an expensive investment. The investment pays back only if client can be retained for a considerable period of time profitably. Companies that look for long term growth and profitability always look to pick the right customer. The right fit means mutual satisfaction, long term association, continued cash flow, client referrals and better employee satisfaction and natural market leadership.

Working with the right clients reduces overall cost of delivery. All organizations fix their cost matrix monitoring their delivery and service organization matrix closely. They seldom look at their sales and marketing teams to trim cost efficiencies. In many

A FAILURE'S REMINISCENCE
LESSONS FROM A LIFETIME OF MANAGEMENT BLUNDERS

companies, cost matrix is best fixed at the procurement end, rather than delivery end.

Wrong clients typically skew the overall cost efficiencies of the enterprise. They pass on their inefficiencies and business immaturity to vendors. If you typically work on a fixed cost model, these are high cost clients. Most companies seldom recognize this aspect of business. Two or three concurrent bad clients have the potential to convert an otherwise cash positive organization into a loss making enterprise.

Any relationship that is mutually appreciative is typically open. When there is better appreciation & forecast of client needs, it becomes easy to manage the ebb and flow of business, especially cash flow. Sudden surges are better handled and any special requests are more easily managed, without costs going through the roof.

One other way to recognize a broken client is to check their payment terms. All businesses have standard payment terms. If an organization promises the moon, with a caveat of longer payment terms, it means you are working with a broken organization. These organizations can seldom be pleased and always have an excuse to refuse payment. Most people seldom walk out of a bad investment.

Immature clients take away a large proportion of management bandwidth.

A FAILURE'S REMINISCENCE
LESSONS FROM A LIFETIME OF MANAGEMENT BLUNDERS

Demanding clients, with little or no respect for vendor operating efficiencies and capabilities, build enormous pressure to deliver on unsustainable challenges. If there is substantial investment in client acquisition, or large payables, managements are forced to bend backward to manage these expectations. Most often these few transactions take a huge toll on management time and contribute to management fatigue.

The litmus test for bad client recognition in your portfolio is to look for employee fatigue in managing the particular account. If your delivery team continuously abhors working on a particular client requirement or your best employees give excuses to avoid a customer or your need to pay an incentive to make your workforce execute a particular order, then it is a client you need to avoid. Most frontline managers pick up their lifelong association with diabetes, ulcers or high blood pressure servicing a particular client, for a very short duration. My experience suggests that better employees quit within six months of bringing on board and continuously managing a single large difficult customer.

The bottom line for every management is to look internally and define the client base they can currently handle. They have to be choosier selecting a client, than they are selecting an employee or a vendor. Any client who can dramatically change your cost efficiencies; disrupt cash flow significantly;

A FAILURE'S REMINISCENCE
LESSONS FROM A LIFETIME OF MANAGEMENT BLUNDERS

cause higher employee turnover; make your teams to work continuously 18 hour days or through weekends for months, without greater reward; and most importantly cannot be a reference anywhere is a customer you better drop or refuse your service. That is the secret to your continued enjoyment managing a business.

LESSONS LEARNT

1. Identify customers to whom we can add a lot of value – they are our best bet to service
2. The DNA of every company is programmed to deliver to particular class of customers – you achieve more success with less stress if you address that customer base
3. Expansion with the right customer base assures long term revenues and lesser cost
4. Be careful to service customers with longer than average payment terms
5. Immature clients take a lot of management bandwidth. Drop these clients, if you can afford it
6. Litmus test of every customer interface is your employee fatigue. If unreasonable customer expectations are killing your team, it means your organization is not the ideal fit for that job

A FAILURE'S REMINISCENCE
LESSONS FROM A LIFETIME OF MANAGEMENT BLUNDERS

"Small Project Teams" Propel Success

One of the common reasons people leave jobs is their perception that they can't grow in the organization. As organizations build systems and mature, roles stabilize. When jobs become routine, average workers grow comfortable performing the role. The highly ambitious find it difficult to adjust to a routine working atmosphere and any sign of monotony scares them away.

It is difficult for managers to constantly provide challenges that the ambitious seek. Many people are resigned to let go good contributors to competition just because the company structure and atmosphere does not support them.

In organizations with a crab framework, it is difficult for new leaders to grow and prosper. There is enough inertia in the system to promote talent. An effective way to help teams navigate the internal apathy is to promote small teams within existing hierarchy.

Companies today face a unique challenge of creating durable systems and processes that is flexible enough to accommodate creative changes. While it looks like an oxymoron at the outset, successful organizations should evolve to create a continuous challenging atmosphere to their employees to deliver high value to their customers

A FAILURE'S REMINISCENCE
LESSONS FROM A LIFETIME OF MANAGEMENT BLUNDERS

One of the most effective ways to engage ambitious employees within a system is to build systems around small teams. This is true not just for project led companies, but also, routine work.

In the case of projects focused companies, the team objectives can easily be defined. There are clearly defined milestones. The milestone achievement is normally defined in terms of time or budget or both. While project milestones are a clear destination, motivation can be further enhanced and work made more interesting by helping the team define and work other linear objectives. These objectives can be focused on either personal improvements or achievement of some other results that evoke a higher level of personal accomplishment in all concerned.

In the case of knowledge industries, defining a career roadmap [from initiation to exit including a clear exit criteria at the time of employment] would help plan transition very easily.

The difficulty is more pronounced in the case of process industries. Companies look at work rotation as a way to kill boredom and infuse change. Production driven cash incentives have a limited value from a motivation perspective, but are a general practice. Companies find it difficult to look beyond.

A FAILURE'S REMINISCENCE
LESSONS FROM A LIFETIME OF MANAGEMENT BLUNDERS

While on the shop floor, production is extremely important, it is always possible to form shop floor teams to look at growth and productivity objectives beyond production.

"Quality Circles" were popular on the shop floor sometime back. Each quality circle defined a problem area through brain storming and worked towards achieving improvement in existing practices using collective experience and statistical quality control techniques.

Managements with a clear plan and productivity focus can engage workers very effectively in these activities. As long as they do not treat it as a fad, and budget to implement effective programs with a clear Return of Investment [ROI], workers' are happy to contribute. Monetary and non-cash incentives as recognition for successful projects can bring a large cumulative process improvements. Improvement programs can be treated as small projects and high energy workers involved in such projects also.

In discrete manufacturing process, each batch can be treated as a small project and its completion can be planned from inception to closure. Team members can be involved in risk identification and mitigation as a first step of the process. Collective identification of risks and clarity on mitigation procedure on occurrence will help production managers avoid many shop floor problems. Rigid attitude of shop floor managers [especially

A FAILURE'S REMINISCENCE
LESSONS FROM A LIFETIME OF MANAGEMENT BLUNDERS

promote managers, who see promotion as an improvement of social status improvement] is a big risk in this endeavour.

Converting routine and boring shop floor activities into interesting and intellectually rewarding project focused activities brings greater team involvement. It is a sure guarantee to retain the smarter members of the team and make life less absorbing to the others.

LESSONS LEARNT
1. Build systems around small teams
2. Building small teams and empowering people will help teams build self-confidence to succeed.
3. Create an atmosphere of continuous challenges, so people stay back to learn. No one gets a feeling that he has outgrown the organization
4. In project focused organizations and discrete manufacturing companies, the team objectives should be backed by specific milestones
5. Engage employees to look beyond production targets and evoke their intelligence

A FAILURE'S REMINISCENCE
LESSONS FROM A LIFETIME OF MANAGEMENT BLUNDERS

Shaping Career - Employer Type Identification

Organizations are a reflection of the personality of their chief executives. Most company policies reflect the identity of their executive, rather than the shared belief of the Board or the employees. Companies re-build their DNA based on the commitments and the expectations that a CEO sets among investors and the time frame he buys to deliver his commitments.

There are two classic sets of drivers in the working of a company. The first is "**economic value driven**" and the second is "**organizational capability driven**".

Economic Value Driven

Economic value is purely revenue and margin focused. The CEO and Board are completely focused to achieve specific annual, quarterly and weekly targets to the exclusivity of everything else. In such organizations, everyone seems to like numbers. Survival and growth is only tracked in terms of currency exclusive to everything else. It is a high – risk, high – reward game. You survive only if you can win consistently and not otherwise. Fast growing organizations have this approach in their DNA and most times are media and analyst darlings. The cost to survive is rather steep. It is not unusual for mid-level executives and first level

A FAILURE'S REMINISCENCE
LESSONS FROM A LIFETIME OF MANAGEMENT BLUNDERS

supervisors to carry the legacy of their tenure through life time ailments.

Executives with smaller execution timeline; or those that have set very high expectations among astute investors; or those that have inherited huge losses and are working to rebuild; or have managements with key executives setting a three or five year deadline to sell the company to other investors from a retirement perspective are likely to lead these companies. They attract people with similar perspectives and the team propels each other. These high energy teams do whatever it takes to meet the business objectives, with less thought to personal or after-life. The laser sharp goals act as a tonic and the monetary rewards justify the addiction.

Organizational Capability Driven

The second type of organization is competency driven. These organizations are more process focused and may have a hierarchy. Organizational maturity and constant learning are buzzwords. Career is defined more in terms of stability driven growth rather than quantum leaps. Exposure to all aspects of business is another trait. "Work – Life Balance" is another important characteristic. These companies are actually an "aspirational employer". They pay moderately, jumps are measured to certain norms, work itself is positioned as an incentive and benefits package exceed monetary rewards in terms of variable pay.

Leaders with a broader vision and an attitude to leave behind a legacy are most likely to head these organizations. Large companies with good balance sheet run by professionals also prefer to manage these kinds of organizations. Small companies in specific niches, or those having technocrat – managers as entrepreneurs, typically build this kind of organizations.

There are some companies that have a measure of both. These are few and far between.

The Employee Perspective

Employees seldom look at a prospective employer from this perspective. For most people, employment decisions rest only on salary & designation. It seems that nothing else seems to matter.

An Economic Value driven organization gives more money, but also expects more deliverable consistently from each employee. An extremely competent, mid – level, career focused individual would find such opportunities exhilarating. These companies would be a good alternative for people wanting to start their own organizations, but having responsibilities that inhibit them from not having a steady income. The same opportunity would positively kill a person

A FAILURE'S REMINISCENCE
LESSONS FROM A LIFETIME OF MANAGEMENT BLUNDERS

who does not have well rounded exposure in his early years, or those who have spent time managing responsibilities not part of their role.

Youngsters, in their formative years, learn more by joining organizational capability driven companies. Anyone looking at a mid – career change or having to balance multiple responsibilities or seeking to come back into organized employment would do well to work in mature organizations.

The trickiest part however is people with two to five years of industry exposure. Most of them believe that they have the knowledge required to push the earth, but sadly destroy them-selves when they get on to the speeding train.

Employer Conundrum

It is the current management fad to speak about removing 10% deadwood every year. Managements believe that talent resides in a bell curve and it is extremely simple to identify the worst performing team members and weed them out. Company hires misfits due to combined immaturity of the hiring team and a lack of understanding the company organizational culture. Every statement about removing deadwood is a direct management admission that they have failed and are nurturing an immature hiring process.

A FAILURE'S REMINISCENCE
LESSONS FROM A LIFETIME OF MANAGEMENT BLUNDERS

If skill is the only barometer to hire a person, then organizational misfits are a given. No organization has any reason to hire wrongly or retain such persons beyond a reasonable tenure, when it is extremely apparent that the person is an organizational misfit.

Human Relations Managers have the most important role to play in the entire process. The recruiter has a responsibility to analyse their companies and the management drivers before shortlisting hiring traits and presenting profiles to hiring managers. Relationships tend to be longer if the shortlisted person matches the organizational profile completely.

If the skill is niche, and organizations do not get matching profiles, it is better to hire the best person as a contractor and let him go after project completion. That induces lesser organizational stress and working environment remains harmonious.

LESSONS LEARNT

1. Understand your executive focus and their drivers for the organization
2. Understand your organizational personality
3. Map the individual's personality to the organizational personality
4. Employees' with lust for money must look to work in number focused organizations – employees' with career focus must choose to work in a process oriented organization

A FAILURE'S REMINISCENCE
LESSONS FROM A LIFETIME OF MANAGEMENT BLUNDERS

Circle of Creativity

As a child, the United States meant Hollywood, Mickey & Donald and Oswald to me. The genius behind these wonderful animation and movies was a man called "Walt Disney". Walt was also the drive behind the theme parks [Disneyland, Water Parks etc] that is a craze in most metropolises today.

Constant lifetime innovation made Walt Disney unique. Management of seemingly unlimited creativity made him a genius. Robert Dilts studied the Walt Disney process on his death in 1968 and built a sustained model for managing creativity. It is the "Circle of Creativity".

For someone like me, who ventured to leave a good job to embrace entrepreneurship and build a business around my innovation, this process was invaluable. For all persons, who dare to dream and build a business based on their ideas, this short note is a "must – read".

Innovation is the new cliché in most organizations. Organizations create highly paid teams to innovate. While that brings focus to an objective, it seldom tracks the intellectual property that delivery teams create.

Managements confuse intellectual property to just patents or product ideas. But innovation goes beyond these obvious definitions. This

A FAILURE'S REMINISCENCE
LESSONS FROM A LIFETIME OF MANAGEMENT BLUNDERS

truth is there is a lot of innovation that happens in delivery teams and that is seldom recorded or even appreciated.

From my perspective, in everyday work, there are many areas, where trained and experienced teams have to identify new ways to achieve the objective. Project managers are best placed to identify the intellectual property individuals create as a part of the project deliverable. In many ways, these seem very obvious at the time of planning. Any part of the proposed solution that is not documented or without ready support activity requires innovation.

Three kinds of people populate delivery teams: Dreamers; Realists; and Critics. Dreamers make innovation happen. Realists establish time frame and milestones with evidence and test procedures. Critics review the need, process and tests and justify the ROI. This is a sequential and iterative process. Managers must understand the process in order to reduce project risks and make innovation happen within time and budget. People identification is extremely crucial.

"Team Dreamers" should ideally be risk takers and should have a combination of architect / designers and young coders, with good basics. The manager's crucial role is to define the end objective with clarity. The team comes back with a roadmap to achieve the objectives. The list all alternatives and

A FAILURE'S REMINISCENCE
LESSONS FROM A LIFETIME OF MANAGEMENT BLUNDERS

test every alternative for results. This team fails more often than they succeed. Every failure tells the team what not to do. It should consider every failure a spring board for success. The attitude is best summed up in the words of Woody Allen – "If you are not failing often, it's a sign you are not doing anything innovative".

"Team Realists" are people who ask the "How to?" questions. They relate the problem statement and suggested technology alternatives to the project. They view solutions with respect to time and space. This team normally reviews schedules for innovation delivery; interfaces; changes, the proposed innovation, has on the entire project; and its effect on the overall project budgets and guidelines. The important thing to note is that this team does not rule out alternatives, but seeks clarity through demos, prototypes, story board etc. The project manager and mature team members form the "Dream Realists". Ideas do not move beyond the two teams till all flags raised by "Team Realist" are resolved by "Team Dreamers".

"Team Critics" play the devil's advocate. They review the proposal for objective, feasibility, risks and completeness. All remaining team members normally form the "Team Critics". "Team Dreamers" come back with solutions and answers to all flags risen at this stage. One of the two things naturally happens. If the proposal is sound, then the

A FAILURE'S REMINISCENCE
LESSONS FROM A LIFETIME OF MANAGEMENT BLUNDERS

best alternatives would be explored further by the dreamers and they come back with better solutions. Alternatively, ideas are dumped and proposals get back to the drawing board.

Walt Disney's process revolutionized the global entertainment industry with evergreen characters and changed the entertainment industry, in much the same way Bill Gates or Steve Jobs changed information technology industry at the end of the century.

An appreciation of the process enables project managers identify, nurture and quantify hidden intellectual property in their projects. Dreamers and achievers contribute to the projects willingly. The teams give them the recognition they deserve. The critics get their opportunity to assess without necessarily curbing the innovation required for success.

Negativism breeds when critics cite experience to frustrate changes. This frustration can reduce dramatically through an organized process of change management.

The 'Circle of creativity" affords a chance for creativity, even while it celebrates dissent. It is a sustainable model to plan change and manage risks in projects with risk of unknown.

A FAILURE'S REMINISCENCE
LESSONS FROM A LIFETIME OF MANAGEMENT BLUNDERS

LESSONS LEARNT

1. Innovation is more than patents. It is about how we arrive at solutions to client problems
2. Every innovation team should have three kinds of members – Dreamers, realists and critics
3. Dreamers identify alternatives and test to rule out alternatives
4. Realists validate alternatives and realistically check the practicability of the alternatives suggested
5. Critics ask all the tough questions that clients, investors, management and other outsiders ask.
6. Critics step in only when Realists clear the solution for review

A FAILURE'S REMINISCENCE
LESSONS FROM A LIFETIME OF MANAGEMENT BLUNDERS

Psychological Market Leadership

Text books define market leadership in terms of market share; percentage of revenue; sales units; or any related sales denomination. Popular business press defines markets and companies by the same yard stick. Our perception of market leadership is a reflection of who is the biggest and / or what percentage of the market a company or products occupy. That is the pure quantification of market presence.

Market leadership implies domination. Physical numbers are a good measure. That is not however the absolute. There is another important aspect to leadership that transcends quantity dimension to market share. That is Thought Leadership.

Thought Leadership reflects the qualitative aspects of leadership. Some products / companies may not be big or have chosen the path of numbers to reflect leadership, but set the trends within the industry. They may either be the cost leaders or the innovation leaders. They set the benchmark for their competitors to run after. They impact all players through their product offerings or bring in a new dimension to business that customers' crave and demand. These set of competencies define the market and make established players change for the better. Companies that are able to influence the market and industry through innovation provide the psychological market leadership.

A FAILURE'S REMINISCENCE
LESSONS FROM A LIFETIME OF MANAGEMENT BLUNDERS

Psychological market leadership is a rare combination of intellectual and implementation leadership.

Implementation Leadership is all about increasing, both, the quality of delivery and profitability. It is a state of leadership where managements scout and introduce best practices into every stage of their delivery process. The process helps accrue value and leads to dramatic cost reduction. Managements should focus extensively on building core competencies within the organization so that they are able to set extremely high delivery standards and commit consistent results to their clients. They examine execution mistakes objectively [not just their team, but others in the industry] and introduce effective safeguards against them. The quality standards and competencies push competition so hard, and so often, that they are forced to adopt or close.

A psychological market leader sets the industry standard and is always the benchmark for competition. They define the industry rules and redefine them periodically at will.

Intellectual leadership is also about introducing newer products and technologies. Many companies relate innovation in terms of dollars spent or patents filed. The real innovation is all about understanding the

A FAILURE'S REMINISCENCE
LESSONS FROM A LIFETIME OF MANAGEMENT BLUNDERS

client needs better and introducing the right technology or product at the appropriate price point. Companies that focus on intellectual leadership do not copy the state-of-the-art, but define the standard. They do not necessarily spend big money on their innovation, but always look for the most appropriate manner to meet a customer's latent needs. The single point objective of all innovation is the customer.

When more than one company pushes the frontier in any industry, innovators eventually stand apart, while the others close shop or merge into the profitable companies. Competition eventually becomes less and business more profitable overall.

Market leadership normally follows Thought Leadership.

Thought Leadership is the cause. Market Leadership is the result.

LESSONS LEARNT

1. Thought leadership is as important as market leadership
2. Market leadership is about the quantitative aspects of business – thought leadership is about qualitative aspect of business
3. Thought leaders define the industry benchmark
4. Thought leaders bring innovation to the forefront and introduce newer technologies
5. Thought leadership results in market leadership

A FAILURE'S REMINISCENCE
LESSONS FROM A LIFETIME OF MANAGEMENT BLUNDERS

Value Pricing Strategy

"Product Value" seems to be a constant mantra on every salesperson's vocabulary. It is one of the wands that pre-suppose many sales. "Value for money" is another word that one hears very often.

One of the most important facets of product pricing is its perceived value. That depends entirely on which segment of the market you are focused on currently. Costs associated with management of each segment are different.

Marketing teams make a mistake identifying product value. It is a disaster to push products at wrong price points. Many times large markets are ignored since managements' lack the necessary innovation to price a product for the segment. Low denomination sachets have transformed many off – the – shelf retail products. Premium products are projected as "value for money" in product advertising. Not just technical entrepreneurs, but even large brands make this mistake often. Large retail chains are forced to close outlets, after bleeding, since they do not understand the value chain where their presence would make a difference.

There are four typical value pricing strategies. The "Money Value" is at the top of the pyramid. This is typically called the "premium segment". These products are focused on wealthy and the discerning. Clients look for the best and would not crib about paying a premium to get what they believe is the best the world has to offer. You tend to compete with global companies in this space. The products have aspiration value and are normally associated with celebrities. Celebrity association is the norm during product introduction. Word of mouth publicity carries the brand to the next stage. Exclusivity sets the product from others. Any product that is available at street corners do not qualify for the premium pricing.

"Value for Money" is a hackneyed term. Value for Money normally means "I get what I pay for" and it is not the cheapest goods in town. This is a typical middle class attitude to getting the best deal for their money. The product range in this segment is vast. The marketer has to justify price versus the features. This is tough selling and would appeal to a large segment of the market. High footfalls and informed selling make a large difference at the time of product introduction and availability is a strong differentiator for repeat sales.

The third part of the paradigm can be best defined as "Value for Many" segment. Customers are concerned about the functionality rather than brand name. Highly evolved clients or people with the need but without the means are typical customers. Online trading portals represent this trend,

A FAILURE'S REMINISCENCE
LESSONS FROM A LIFETIME OF MANAGEMENT BLUNDERS

since the belief is that the web provides an easy comparison platform.

Service or products purchased not for personal consumption, but to meet the needs of their clients, employees or for statutory purposes are good candidates for this pricing model.

The most important category globally is defined as the "Price Point Value". People buy if the product value is apparent and need is immediate. People do not spend unnecessarily if the need is not pressing. Small retail quantities and discount hunting are the norms in this market. Providing absolutely necessary features at the right price point in the immediate neighbourhood is the way to approach this market.

Strategic teams make the mistake of wrongly defining their client. The common marketing problem is an appreciation of who benefits from their offering the most.

The first challenge is to define the customer and more importantly list the characteristics / needs that make him accept to use the product / service for a fair price.

The second challenge is to create a marketing strategy that will help us only reach the person and not anyone else. I see sales guys getting excited about a larger market and lose focus on the intended segment. This may give some relationship

A FAILURE'S REMINISCENCE
LESSONS FROM A LIFETIME OF MANAGEMENT BLUNDERS

based success initially, but would drain the organization eventually.

The third challenge is to tailor the delivery mechanism, product or service offering and the execution metrics to meet the exact needs of the target market. Operational teams compare their delivery standards to the best in business and plan systems that would make like comparisons favourable. It may not always be necessary to provide every alternative that the competition offers. The most logical alternatives for that segment would be the optimum standards that one should seek. Creating a delivery metrics from that perspective would be more logical and would reduce the chances of failure.

LESSONS LEARNT

1. Identifying the right product value is the first marketing challenge
2. "Money Value – Value for Money – Value for Many – Price Point Value" are the four alternatives that marketers should be aware of
3. Identify which customer benefits most from our product
4. Build a service organization that meets the delivery requirement of that customer

A FAILURE'S REMINISCENCE
LESSONS FROM A LIFETIME OF MANAGEMENT BLUNDERS

Should succession be a race?

All companies have to see personnel changes. Most often, when things are going well and people are delivering, it seems that there is no need to look beyond the person. In many small and medium organizations, the key persons often tend to look irreplaceable.

However, for organizations to survive and grow the early leaders, and even more importantly to retain and motivate people, providing a career path is necessary. Career path implies selecting persons to move to a higher role and moulding them over a period of time to step into the bigger shoes. This is not just true for the top management role, but also for junior positions. When people understand what they need to do to grow and move up their career, they are motivated to succeed and help others grow.

The philosophy is as true to government, political parties, terrorist organizations and the non-government sector, as it is to corporate bodies.

Succession planning is not a foreign concept to many organizations. Large global companies realize that it is a crucial risk mitigation strategy and incorporate it in their organizational development structures. Many family run organizations realize that a good succession plan is an absolute must to restrain the younger elements from reaching the court and groom people rather early.

A FAILURE'S REMINISCENCE
LESSONS FROM A LIFETIME OF MANAGEMENT BLUNDERS

However even within these progressive organizations, seldom does one see efforts to initiate this concept at the operations level. This is an equally important spoke that can help the wheel rotate easily.

When organizations groom people, one notices that they end up choosing a few candidates for mentoring to the higher role. This is not bad, since disasters can be better managed through that principle. I have known companies which identify different persons to take on the responsibility depending on the amount of time they have at their disposal. It is not uncommon to consider different persons for different eventualities in case of emergencies.

The success of this program is not about the eventual successor, but about the people who were not considered. It happens most times that the company loses most of these best persons to the competition. It does not seem a wise decision to mentor people and build their competencies over a fairly large period of time to only lose them at short notice and handicap the eventual winner.

One way to avoid the "winner's curse" is to be transparent about motives and be realistic about opportunities. It pays to let people know what their chances and set the expectations in a clear manner as and when they reach pre-decided milestones.

A FAILURE'S REMINISCENCE
LESSONS FROM A LIFETIME OF MANAGEMENT BLUNDERS

People appreciate the investments the company is making to enable them to increase their breadth of experience. At each stage, when appraisals are honest and realistic, and people are given opportunities to get over mistakes and disappointments, they tend to tone their own expectations and learn to be happy at the pace of their own growth.

In a growing organization, managements can always look for ways and means to engage a person at a higher level of responsibility. As long as the Board or the Management communicate that the person is wanted and always has a role to play beyond a designation, there will be understanding and co-operation, once the initial denial stage is overcome.

Communicating to a person the reason why someone else is a better match for a particular position, as early as possible, and giving realistic career alternatives to the person and enabling the person to grow into the alternative is the best way to retain your best people after the tough decisions are taken.

Even more importantly, the tendency to form camps and hedge your own future on the progress of another person would reduce dramatically. Everyone would focus on the betterment of the organization, rather than plotting their own survival.

A FAILURE'S REMINISCENCE
LESSONS FROM A LIFETIME OF MANAGEMENT BLUNDERS

LESSONS LEARNT

1. Succession planning is a requirement for every organization
2. It is necessary to develop multiple persons for every role
3. When opportunities actually arise, only one person can be elevated
4. In order not to lose others to competition, it is necessary to define expectations early and keep everyone in the loop regarding individual progress
5. Letting people know the logic behind decisions, helps them realign their objectives after the initial shock and ensures that they continue to deliver continuously

A FAILURE'S REMINISCENCE
LESSONS FROM A LIFETIME OF MANAGEMENT BLUNDERS

Continuous success needs abandonment

There is a popular saying "Don't repair what is not broken". This adage may not always be true for organizations.

All successful organizations have one or more businesses that bring in the revenue. This is the cash cow. Organizations identify themselves through these businesses. Like everything in life, businesses have a life of their own. Businesses find it difficult to scale rapidly once they approach revenue maturity. After a point, the profitability starts shrinking or remains the same. At this stage, every business needs redefinition of their offering to sustain the market share. If that can't be done, managements need to kill the business to prevent stakeholder misery.

Managements seldom consider killing a business. Every cash cow becomes a holy cow. The track record of the business over the last decade or the image of the company is the popular rational one hears to sustain a has-been business. The real reason why this hard step is seldom taken is due to a fear of unknown or fear of failure or emotional baggage attached with the success or all of them.

History points out at even large organizations [among the Fortune 100] that have been consigned to history books due to this

A FAILURE'S REMINISCENCE
LESSONS FROM A LIFETIME OF MANAGEMENT BLUNDERS

management failure. 84 Fortune 100 companies in 1900 no longer exist.

In every era, products and services become extinct due to changes in customer behaviour, need changes or technology obsolesce. Products and solutions that meet today's requirements may not necessarily meet the aspirations of tomorrow's clients. In a dynamic organization, the management always has to focus its strategic intent on tomorrow's need and its execution intent on today's challenges.

When management vision tunnels to tomorrow's needs, it happens that many of the pillars that have been the reason for today's success may not be important factors for tomorrow. Attitudes, products, people or process that has ensured our today's success may actually impede tomorrow's survival.

A solution plan for the immediate long term is seldom a destructive evolution, but a gradual evolution of process, methods, products or solutions. It happens that the solution will grow gradually to meet higher standards of acceptance. A proper definition of the long term vision normally helps management define an evolutionary pathway to the ultimate goal. Managements can intervene to change today's success factors to be relevant tomorrow.

Identification and planned abandonment of waste in short, but successive iterations is a

A FAILURE'S REMINISCENCE
LESSONS FROM A LIFETIME OF MANAGEMENT BLUNDERS

sure way to rid the system of inefficiencies. A firm but understanding attitude helps them get over factors that inhibit such change. Large changes are always difficult to implement. Small, but purposeful changes seldom attract much attention and ensure quick compliance.

Companies that practice planned abandonment continuously examine all aspects of their business – people, process, markets, products and attitudes – from a position of their current relevance to the client requirement and solution cost. They are able to identify all practices that do not add value to client and build sloth in the system. They need to build systems, processes and a mind-set that promotes continuous improvement through better methods and materials and through constant learning / unlearning. Constant value accretion is the only guarantee against any obsolescence.

Removing waste is a challenge in most situations since there always is a baggage attached to present practices. Maintaining a status quo is always a much simpler than monitoring change. However it is a necessary evil to guarantee continuous margins. When small changes happen all the time, people are constantly learning new things. The cost of training is small and in many cases is a part of daily life. In such circumstances, change happens without much friction.

A FAILURE'S REMINISCENCE
LESSONS FROM A LIFETIME OF MANAGEMENT BLUNDERS

When managements have neglected planned abandonment, they have to bite the bullet at a stage when things become really hot. At that stage, rational decisions bring along unimaginable pain to every stakeholder.

LESSONS LEARNT

1. Beyond a point, revenues stabilize but costs continue to spiral for all products
2. Every product has a life span.
3. Management's strategic intent must be on tomorrow's need and execution on today's challenges
4. A clear product or solution vision helps build an evolutionary product path
5. It helps to kill waste and abandon all process / features that don't work. What survives are the best practices
6. The quicker managements learn to abandon waste, lesser the pain to all stakeholders

A FAILURE'S REMINISCENCE
LESSONS FROM A LIFETIME OF MANAGEMENT BLUNDERS

Software career evolution – A perspective

Career progression is a vexed question for many technical folks. The power of leadership and becoming the boss seems a natural progression for most young professionals. I have had instances where young developers have come to me seeking a designation change, since their parents' are planning marriage.

I write this during the appraisal cycle, so young professionals can understand themselves better and choose a career path that best suits their competencies. You may want to read this if you believe that your career path has hit a roadblock and your magic touch vanished with your last promotion.

There are broadly three kinds of career paths, before a developer – technology; product management; and operations management.

The technology option is mostly for the geeks. If you love technology for its own sake, and prefer to spend your waking hours tweaking that new application or trying to address a technology problem posted on a blog, you qualify. Most geeks I know are warm human beings and enjoy a joke. It might surprise you, but anyone in this career path earns roughly twice or thrice what a manager earns, over a lifetime.

A FAILURE'S REMINISCENCE
LESSONS FROM A LIFETIME OF MANAGEMENT BLUNDERS

All persons who opt for the technology path are very good programmers. They grow to design sub-systems and then become technology architects. Very few technical architects get a chance to do solution architecture. Working within a few domains helps understand client needs better and enable faster professional growth.

Product management is basically customer focused. This stream is for all those persons who enjoy client interaction and interface. You need to enjoy travel; keep in touch with technology [the buzz words at-least]; and communicate effectively to make your mark. I would suggest this career path for all those developers who dived into coding hoping to see the world and for the worldly pleasures a software career implies. Technology sales, pre-sales, proposal writing, business analysis and technology implementation roles are some of the more visible faces of product management. There are hundreds of young professionals providing remote technology support in call centres. If you are lucky to be in a service organization, onsite co-ordination is a definite possibility.

More than technology, you need to sharpen your linguistic and communication skills to succeed in product management. Your employer will consider you for this role, only if you have demonstrated a history of tact and polish in your dealings with the team and client in your current role.

A FAILURE'S REMINISCENCE
LESSONS FROM A LIFETIME OF MANAGEMENT BLUNDERS

If you are living your dad's [or mom's] dream of being an IT professional and not because you like programming, then becoming an operations manager is your lot. You can begin by being an elder brother to your juniors and mentor them and slowly grow into a project manager. You need to code well, if you want respect from people who report to you. That is however optional, if you are a good party animal with nice listening skills.

The lot of the project managers is the worst. Their pay scale plateau fastest. They face client and management bullets. Their job is to defend decisions they are not responsible for. They hand-out geometrical pay hikes to their team members, when their own salary sees an arithmetic increase. Becoming a project manager is not necessarily the best option in the software industry.

While everyone likes a promotion, you need to be careful to seek one. Many companies dish out designations, if that is an option to avoid a pay hike. If you are not ready to manage the responsibilities that the promotion brings along with the designation change, then your career comes to a stop.

Ask yourself a thousand times, if you really need that promotion letter. It could be your ticket for lifetime use of anti – BP, anti – diabetes or anti – ulcer drugs, if sought at an inappropriate time.

A FAILURE'S REMINISCENCE
LESSONS FROM A LIFETIME OF MANAGEMENT BLUNDERS

LESSONS LEARNT

1. There are three software career paths – technical, client facing and managerial
2. Technology career path [developer – designer – architect] path is the most rewarding in terms of remuneration over a lifetime.
3. Client facing paths give you opportunities to see the world and face myriad challenges
4. Managerial careers plateau fastest, with arithmetic pay hikes and little to show by way of promotions
5. Managers have to face clients, management and team ire constantly

A FAILURE'S REMINISCENCE
LESSONS FROM A LIFETIME OF MANAGEMENT BLUNDERS

Who Should Review Your Business Plans

New business opportunities are a different kettle of worms. Entrepreneurs build Business Plan mostly at the instance of their financiers – top management, bankers, VC, government agencies etc. Very rarely do people spend good time to build a plan for their own purpose. Business plan is normally reviewed by "experienced folks (!!!)".

Most objections during the review of new business plans come from our individual experience of our existing business. Another barometer to assess every opportunity is its relation to how a business performed in the last boom or era and why it will fail in the current scenario. I have a lot of my ideas rubbished by well-meaning people, since it has failed in the past. Negative review feedbacks seldom weaken the resolve of persons with a passion for the project.

Every business has its own opportunities and challenges. Each risk has its own probability of occurrence and method to manage them. Our own experiences may not necessarily reflect the true worth of the new opportunity and the ability of new persons to handle them. Individual experiences definitely help identify risks and create a strong mitigation strategy. But they should not necessarily be the sole basis of a decision.

A FAILURE'S REMINISCENCE
LESSONS FROM A LIFETIME OF MANAGEMENT BLUNDERS

The focus during review of a business plan must necessarily be the components that will make it functional and a success. The possibility of success increases when the plan is reviewed by different kinds of reviewers from different perspectives.

The best persons to do the initial review would be sympathetic colleagues, close friends and family who understand the business. They are needed as moral support to keep your morale high and for no other reason.

The plan itself should be evolved during discussions with two critical stakeholders – probable clients and vendors. External stakeholders who can make a difference to the business bring different perspectives to the plan. They are the best persons to validate the assumptions. There is no better way to help identify solution alternatives, material alternatives or pricing strategies and prepare to set the right expectations during the launch.

Vendor reviews become useful when they start identifying alternatives from a value and cost perspective. Value definition is a parameter most vendor discussions never move towards. Specialists in every area are exposed to more alternatives in their area than any designer can possibly phantom. Creative individuals can suggest myriad alternatives to the same problem that will reduce design and sourcing complications and costs.

A FAILURE'S REMINISCENCE
LESSONS FROM A LIFETIME OF MANAGEMENT BLUNDERS

Client intrinsic needs are well articulated in conversations. Product costs are almost always linked to the extrinsic needs. Mapping the need statement to the product cost and identifying the segment that will buy the product at that price point is the final guarantor of success of the business plan. External discussions with this perspective, rather than on likely success of the plan, will be more useful in the long run. The best way to determine that your discussions are not cosmetic is to ask the client to give you a "letter of intent" to help him build the product and test it at your client premises without any obligation to buy. If the customer bites the bullet and signs up, you have a potential business plan that works.

A trusted Chartered Account gives good insight into the taxation aspects of a plan. If you can plan the basic components of the plan and its relative cost, they will be helpful in arriving at the probable P & L account. It is advisable to be extremely realistic of the assumptions and its probable chance to happen when the numbers are put together. Just pulling numbers on a spread-sheet is a favoured option, but does not help you actually arrive at the ROI scenario or appreciate the "GO – NO GO" scenario that your investor or patron is looking for.

Look for senior industry experts, and check the plan with them, from a perspective of their participation as a Chief Operating

A FAILURE'S REMINISCENCE
LESSONS FROM A LIFETIME OF MANAGEMENT BLUNDERS

Officer or Head – Sales or whatever. Even if they show disinterest, they will add a lot of value with their background and expertise on the feasibility of the assumptions. It is always extremely difficult to get people to sign – on to a start – up. Don't be embarrassed or disturbed, if people refuse. You may not even be able to pay their salaries at this stage, and their refusal is actually not a bad result.

The most common reaction I have seen from entrepreneurs is to take every such negative response personally. This is not necessary. People may have a million reasons not to join a start – up. Refusal to work in a start – up is not a personal refusal to work with you.

One way an industry veteran may help you is by identifying sub – contracting opportunities. These may not be on your immediate radar, when you plan a business, but can be vital cash boosters to a start – up. These sub – contracting opportunities also push you to understand the existing quality bench marks in competitor companies.

Once you put the plan is place, it is always advisable to seek the branch managers of three or four banks and request them for a loan based on the plan you have put together. It is always better to go to conservative, private banks and extremely large process oriented banks for the review. Small, private bankers are normally trained

A FAILURE'S REMINISCENCE
LESSONS FROM A LIFETIME OF MANAGEMENT BLUNDERS

to look at the business from entrepreneur's perspective, while the large process oriented banks measure your plan from a host of metrics that insulate failure. If they offer the loan, then it means that your plan can stand the test of a critical review. If they reject, you can always ask them what needs to be done to improve chances of getting a loan and you will get free advice. As long as you have an open mind, you will learn a lot in the process.

With all these reviews, remember that Business Plans are paper tools. In real life, things may not pan in much the same way as we plan. It helps to have alternative plans in place, if environment changes or some other issue prevents you from executing your plan.

My entrepreneurial journey, so far, has shown that the alternate business plan is what normally pans out in the end.

LESSONS LEARNT

1. Don't feel shy to have your business plan validated by many persons
2. A probable customer will validate your pricing and delivery / product specifications. If you get a LOI, then your plan works.
3. A vendor can bring alternate materials / practice / operating procedure to the table. A helpful vendor can even introduce clients.
4. A chartered accountant checks on the taxation assumptions and pricing and probable P&L assumptions.
5. An industry veteran, would come back with their own assessment on the applicability, when you check their interest to work as a senior executive in the proposed start - up

A FAILURE'S REMINISCENCE
LESSONS FROM A LIFETIME OF MANAGEMENT BLUNDERS

6. A bank / investor as the last port of call can validate all the above. If they offer to invest or lend money, then your business plan is worth investing on
7. Have an alternate business plan in place – just in case your original plan does not pan out.

A FAILURE'S REMINISCENCE
LESSONS FROM A LIFETIME OF MANAGEMENT BLUNDERS

Encourage employees to fire their boss

It is said that employees work for the company, but leave due to their bosses. In any service organization, a knowledge worker walks out with experience every evening. The competency a person brings to the table comes from the experience in the job he has been recruited for.

Workers hungry for growth always look to increase the breadth and depth of their experience. Most companies provide multiple hats for workers to gain expertise.

All organizations have enthusiastic volunteers, who take responsibilities beyond their normal call of duties. They rush to help when possible. Organizations also have individuals who deliver what they have promise, but seldom over - reach themselves. Some persons wait for precise guidance to deliver results. Whatever the nature of the person, the expectation of the individual, from the organization, is almost the same.

Enthusiastic persons contribute their might. The results may not be the optimum, since they may not be the subject matter experts. People who fear failure seldom step out of their comfort zone. In all cases, constant guidance and training is a requirement.

A FAILURE'S REMINISCENCE
LESSONS FROM A LIFETIME OF MANAGEMENT BLUNDERS

Large companies with substantial training budgets offer training programs for its own sake. Training without a goal is a wasted experience. Providing career direction and annual goals and building programs to help a person meet the goal most times make the knowledge gaining experience more rewarding. Training related to work goals builds organizational competencies.

The other key aspect in the whole exercise is the value that a boss brings to the table in the knowledge curve. A person with practical, hands-on experience is almost always respected and looked up to. An organization culture that encourages failure helps build mutual confidence in persons. In such organizations, people higher up the hierarchy see themselves as facilitators and problem solvers. The only job they do is to remove all hurdles that help the worker focus on delivering results.

The manager's relationship and intensity of interaction varies with the need. A high performing worker mostly needs a pat on the back. People working at an unhurried pace needs a higher level of motivation to deliver more optimum results. A straggler needs hands-on training in a manner that he can see results for the effort put in. The reporting manager should be the person who provides that hands - on training. Any person who can ungrudgingly give such training gets the employee's support and respect for life.

A FAILURE'S REMINISCENCE
LESSONS FROM A LIFETIME OF MANAGEMENT BLUNDERS

A person who can manage the external stakeholders, appreciate and empathize with the challenges the workers face and cease to be a nuisance on the working floor is the best positioned to lead a team.

Transparency in decision making reduces personnel friction. When everyone understands that there is decency and trust in the system, managers tends to open up and work with their team. If the system encourages each person to kill the aspirations of another to grow, then the environment produces either a toxic mix of ego and politics or encourages a person to opt out.

A mature environment encourages feedback from all sources. A negative feedback is most sought after, since it encourages the individual to correct his faults and become better. In all situations, people must be bothered if they do not get a feedback. It just means that people no longer relate to you and your relationships are extremely artificial.

In an environment, where managers can hand hold a straggler; where training is need based and focuses on results; where transparency in decision making reduces personnel conflict; and where disagreements and negative feedback does not lead to the killing of the messenger; employees walk up and say that they would like to work with a person with higher competency, if they find

A FAILURE'S REMINISCENCE
LESSONS FROM A LIFETIME OF MANAGEMENT BLUNDERS

that they have outgrown the knowledge base of their superior. This is a most welcome situation. You have a chance to improve the competencies of an existing manager and retain the worker. In a situation where that freedom is not there, the worker fires his boss, and also the organization.

LESSONS LEARNT

1. Training without a learning goal is a wasteful exercise
2. Transparency in decision making reduces personnel conflict
3. Disagreements and negative feedback should be encouraged from a perspective of clarifying end objectives
4. Employees must be encouraged to speak – up when they believe that they have over reached the knowledge threshold of their boss
5. Competency should be the corner stone of respect – not just age

A FAILURE'S REMINISCENCE
LESSONS FROM A LIFETIME OF MANAGEMENT BLUNDERS

View your business as a customer

For a committed individual, a business has a lot of emotional connect. The ownership makes us blind to some of our inherent strengths and weakness. The pride makes it difficult to criticize ourselves. The commitment makes it difficult to change. Over a period of time, we lose perspective to the business – we make our businesses a child of our own experiences.

Businesses are meant for a sole purpose – to service the customer. The customer, whether internal or external, justifies our time and assures us a reasonable life style. Every customer's perspective of our business is very different from our own. They look at it from a lesser degree of emotion, but with more criticality, since they are paying us for our efforts. A reasonable and mature customer's perspective adds a large value to our efforts. Their measured criticism identifies areas where we can add value.

Many customers are actually in an extremely good position to help us. They may contribute a lot, if they are from the same industry or understand our business better. The only thing we need to do is go and ask. Most times, we hesitate to ask because we believe he may be uncomfortable or take the effort negatively. From experience, most times I see that my client relationship improves when we sincerely implement their suggestions. Putting together a probable client list and defining an improvement agenda during the meeting helps get better results. It would be worth every cent you spend on the client's lunch.

My experience also suggests that you should respect the person from whom you are seeking advice. You should have an open mind when they speak and be more than open to implement suggestions if you are convinced that it is in everybody's interest. Getting back to the client with an improvement time frame and communicating status, including possible hurdles, helps the client respect us and our business.

Having said that, it must be understood that no customer is able to empathize our situation or problems in a manner we ourselves can. The best people who can suggest changes are we ourselves.

A client looks at our business from three perspectives – [1] how much smarter we can deliver results; [2] how much more value we can bring to the table; and [3] is there scope to reduce costs.

An ability to constantly look at our business from this perspective helps us to deliver better to the customer. An "outside – in" perspective always means asking difficult questions with an open mind. It does not mean being critical about everyone and everything around us, but being more

A FAILURE'S REMINISCENCE
LESSONS FROM A LIFETIME OF MANAGEMENT BLUNDERS

observant to what is happening and how we are doing business

An "outside – in" perspective is to constantly question if our final product / solution is the best we can give in the circumstances. Having a clear product / service improvement goal within a reasonably well defined time frame helps us move beyond operations and its problems to think creatively out of the box. It forces us to look for newer, cheaper or better alternatives to what we currently deliver. Every small incremental result improves our odds to fight inertia, boredom and failure

Another area where we can focus in our search for better solutions comes from our process and systems. Our workplace provides a hundred small, but significant areas to improve productivity and reduce costs. Constant vendor discussions and an open mind help us identify newer products or ideas that we may not be aware of. Product innovations in unrelated areas many times give us opportunities to implement similar concepts in our business. These interactions help us abandon yesterday's perspectives and embrace new realities.

The other important aspect of the "outside – in" perspective is to be your client's vocal representative within your organization. When someone from our team walks and complains about a difficult customer, the natural tendency is to rubbish the client.

A FAILURE'S REMINISCENCE
LESSONS FROM A LIFETIME OF MANAGEMENT BLUNDERS

However if we can stop and reason why the client is seeking what he is, we may be able to understand the situation better. If we can practice this consistently on an organizational plane, lifetime customer loyalty is guaranteed

LESSONS LEARNT

1. Most business are a child of their promoter's sole experience
2. Ask customers' for help to deliver better, if they understand our business well - Have an open mind when a client gives improvement suggestions
3. "Outside – in" perspective to business involves looking at our business from a client perspective
4. Identify hundreds of small changes that can be implemented and keep making positive changes. That builds a strong case against inertia
5. Be the customer's representative within your team – don't rubbish a difficult customer before your team

A FAILURE'S REMINISCENCE
LESSONS FROM A LIFETIME OF MANAGEMENT BLUNDERS

Have delivery teams face customers

Customer facing teams are a part of many businesses. Smart men and women who can communicate well are an extremely important part of an organization. In service organizations in the business – to – business space, you have a specialist role called the business analyst to handle the customers.

Companies avoid having everyone communicate directly with the customer for a variety of reasons. Immature sales and delivery commitments is most common. Legal reasons are another. Hiding unsophisticated delivery teams is the third. Fear of miscommunication is always a justification. Process immaturity is the common thread.

One of the key building blocks of increasing business process maturity is increasing and standardizing business communication among all stakeholders. Business communication includes both formal inter – office and external communication. Every employee must know what to communicate and what to avoid. More importantly, all stakeholders must be involved in internal decision making on key questions where their performance decides the results.

Two biggest advantages of having the delivery team directly interface with the customer are feedback and trust building.

A FAILURE'S REMINISCENCE
LESSONS FROM A LIFETIME OF MANAGEMENT BLUNDERS

Your delivery team learns fast what works and what fails. The learning process is shortened and quality quickly improves. If you have an able manager leading the process, the maturity enhancement cycle reduces dramatically. Internal ego wars and communication gaps reduce since everyone is now on the firing line. An invisible hierarchy builds when any privileged team exclusively does customer interaction. Managing the privilege itself becomes a project. Any individual blunder caused by an individual leads to a larger catastrophe. When a larger team interacts, and a communication hierarchy is built, individual communications and failings can be better managed. Human nature to take ownership for one's own commitment means that the level of operations management changes. People down the line automatically take ownership for their own deliveries and go beyond the call of duty.

Customer trusts when information comes from authentic source. The customer is sure about the status of the order. If there are delivery issues that may cause changes to his plan, he is able to get the feel very early. Managements take customer interface a lot more seriously than they would from one of their subordinates. All problems that generally come from operational inertia from the staff organization will be attended on priority.

A FAILURE'S REMINISCENCE
LESSONS FROM A LIFETIME OF MANAGEMENT BLUNDERS

Clients today employ an online customer dashboard to facilitate the process. In all cases, where there is an organic relationship between the deliveries of the two companies, it helps to streamline the communication without an intense human interface. Real time information can be provided online and customer can always be aware of the latest status of their deliveries. In addition to business – to – business communication, in any situation where there is a discrete transaction, an online dashboard is a boon.

In cases where personal communication is necessary, internal teams must be encouraged to plan the dialogue. All discussions must focus on problems customers face. Teams must be encouraged to speak facts. If the scope of discussion is beyond the scope of the team's ability to handle, the team must let the customer know that the issue must be escalated. The team must give a time frame to have a higher authority speak with the customer. They must internally have the concerned person speak to the client within the time frame.

Identifying areas of improvement is another scope for a direct client interaction. As long as we are prepared to listen [and not judge], a customer's feedback is invaluable. Many suggestions can be easily implemented within a reasonable time. A genuine fear is that customer may hold us accountable for non – implementation of ideas. Customer decision makers understand that not every opinion can be implemented. The dialogue gives us an opportunity to hold back the customer if the feedback is genuine and absence of action would compel the client to move anyway.

It is important for your delivery team to interface also with vendors and other drivers in the market. It is worth having key delivery persons spend time on the websites of your competitors to know what is happening in the industry. The whole process is liberating for the employee and the company.

LESSONS LEARNT

1. Companies avoid having everyone communicate with customers.
2. Fear of unsophisticated communication, legal issues and immature communication are the basic fears.
3. Improve and standardize business communication for every employee.
4. Build processes to ensure that bad news is communicated early
5. Employee enablement builds long term client confidence
6. It is also one way to ensure that clients don't walk out due to any single employee's misjudgement

A FAILURE'S REMINISCENCE
LESSONS FROM A LIFETIME OF MANAGEMENT BLUNDERS

Comprehensive contracts reduce risks

Contracts are the lifeline of any business. Most contracts are drawn keeping the legal requirements in mind. Attorneys draft contracts keeping in mind the litigation aspects. Large companies roll out standard contracts where the terms and conditions for most business transactions are either same or extremely similar.

Contracts must be designed to enable a contract to succeed rather than get into the litigation cycle. Badly designed contracts make attorneys rich, with both parties losing in the bargain.

Success focused contracts must cover four extremely important points, in addition to the standard legalese.

The first and foremost part that needs to be covered is the actual scope of work, with time frame, if possible. The scope of work must be as detailed as possible. The more detailed the scope of work, the less likely the project can fail. All underlying assumptions and exceptions must be very clearly documented. Drawings, samples, prototypes and any other information used to clarify the scope of work must be a part of the contract. Attorneys abhor including all these information in standard contracts for two reasons — the time required to draft contracts become long and size of the

A FAILURE'S REMINISCENCE
LESSONS FROM A LIFETIME OF MANAGEMENT BLUNDERS

contract may not justify the cost of drafting the contract. In such a situation, it is necessary for the end user – the actual customer within the client company - to spend the time to validate the scope of work and the legal team to build the contract around the mutually approved scope of work. Time frame for complete project completion and intermediate mile stones are best defined as closely as possible. This is easy in every contract that runs in project mode. Vendors prefer to keep the details as opaque as possible to help them get execution freedom or reduce costs, while clients may not be bothered about the process as long as delivery is assured. Irrespective of clauses on client inspections or payment schedules, it helps build confidence among customers if the project progress has visibility. Clients can evaluate and manage risks better when they know what is actually happening on the project.

During the execution of the project, it happens that there are external variables to the project. Any variations due to the external factors will basically beyond the vendor's ability to manage. In a classical situation the client may say that the onus of a turnkey project is on the vendor and it is for the vendor to manage the situation. In reality, vendor's failure is actually the project failure and client suffers, irrespective of the penalty clauses. It helps if the vendor can be open about such dependencies during negotiations and the risk mitigation strategy

A FAILURE'S REMINISCENCE
LESSONS FROM A LIFETIME OF MANAGEMENT BLUNDERS

he will adopt to reduce risk of non – performance. The probability of failure, risk and cost sharing in such a situation and terms that the vendor has to insert in their vendor contracts to insulate the project of such risks are key elements of the contract. A legal clause arms the vendor to execute a back – to – back clause with the sub – vendors to reduce project risks. Many vendors need such protection clauses to prod stronger sub – vendors to agree to the terms.

The second key aspect of contracts relates to product acceptability. Acceptance criteria have to be very clearly defined. If the criteria can be quantified and / or test cases simulated, then it is even better. Having an opaque criteria or a flow down of the scope of work does not guarantee a smooth acceptance. It is quite possible the client would focus on functionality during the scope definition and performance or implementation issues would become a show stopper. A quantified acceptance process will ensure that the vendor adopts the same criteria as a part of their internal quality assurance and testing process.

The last, but most important aspect is definition of failure. What constitutes a project failure to the client must be as explicitly defined as possible. This may seem tricky, but every business opportunity flows from a need. The need, if external, would harm or hurt the client substantially.

A FAILURE'S REMINISCENCE
LESSONS FROM A LIFETIME OF MANAGEMENT BLUNDERS

Definition of failure, identifying causative aspects of failures, risks that may cause failure and mitigation strategies in such an event, escalation strategy when such risks occur and strategy to apportion losses in case of such failure is vital to preventing failure

End of the day, every failed project is a waste. Spending time defining the scope, assumptions, risks, acceptance and failure would lead to a 'win – win' situation.

LESSONS LEARNT

1. Design contracts to enable project success – they must out grow from being a legal template
2. The scope of work must be covered in as much detail as possible. Better the definition of SOW, more chances that the project will end as envisaged
3. Begin with defining the timelines – not just end dates, but as many intermediate timelines as feasible
4. Define all external variables as possible. Even in turnkey projects, the onus of management remains on the client and not the vendor.
5. Define acceptance criteria in as much detail as possible
6. Define failure – clearly mention what situation is considered a project failure. If this can be done quite early in project, project clarity flows

A FAILURE'S REMINISCENCE
LESSONS FROM A LIFETIME OF MANAGEMENT BLUNDERS

Business is about exploiting opportunities

It is said that business is all about solving customer problems. Businesses that focus on solving customer current issues or reduce costs are basically working on the status – quo. They work on well perceived customer needs that hopefully attract a lot of other companies to be in same market place. Cutting cost and increasing the breadth of offerings are the typical client acquisition strategies. Most laggards find it difficult to grow fast and profitably in such a scenario. Existing service providers take a substantial part of the business.

Companies become market leaders by exploiting opportunities and not building on a status quo. Building on opportunities means that the customer must be convinced that the vendor can deliver consistent value and the service / product has a definite and quantifiable 'Return on Investment'. The value must be demonstrable in terms of performance. Business only builds when the market accepts value. Companies make money when their business offering has something of real value to a client or market.

The definition of value offering implies that there is a definite unique selling proposition or unique product proposition that the customer can appreciate. The innovation can be in approach, process or solution, but should attack the core of a customer's

A FAILURE'S REMINISCENCE
LESSONS FROM A LIFETIME OF MANAGEMENT BLUNDERS

lacunae in their current business practice. Any solution that complements our current competencies and helps us deliver quality consistently is a sure winner.

When we speak about exploiting existing business opportunities, it does not mean that we should take a piece of work where our competencies are weak or we have to depend on external actors to deliver our client commitments. If the current team cannot deliver with a short learning curve, then the business is not worth coveting for. One can always hire a team to deliver, but the risks of assuming that such a team will ramp up and build on customer expectations is a long shot. We have our credibility at stake to take on a high – risk project.

Merely because a particular solution has helped another company grow, does not necessarily mean that we can succeed in new business. The DNA, competencies and historical opportunities between two entities is different and the success of one entity does not necessarily guarantee the success of another.

In order to identify the most relevant customer problems and map the opportunity with our internal competencies, it is most necessary that our best persons are at client site. In many cases, the best persons always manage the current fire and a dis – spirited sales person is our calling card. If we internally ensure that all our key managers

A FAILURE'S REMINISCENCE
LESSONS FROM A LIFETIME OF MANAGEMENT BLUNDERS

and smart delivery persons meet and identify one new business opportunity that they can define, get a customer acceptance for ROI and sell internally on product delivery every quarter, we have a healthy pipeline of business to nurture and grow.

The solutions does not necessarily need to be a new business, but can be a variable of our existing product line or the applicability of our current solutions to a new set of customers. That is a far more well-meaning and profitable expertise.

It is not necessarily to cut costs and corners to get business and make money. Innovation around our own strengths and circumstances are really the key to new business and logical success.

Once can bring low margin business or undersell only if you can kill competition and rule the industry for a long term. In any other situation, you will drain the company of its competitive energy and investor's money through this business strategy.

A FAILURE'S REMINISCENCE
LESSONS FROM A LIFETIME OF MANAGEMENT BLUNDERS

LESSONS LEARNT

1. New companies gain market share by exploring opportunities and not be offering similar services as an existing customer
2. Demonstrate that the offering brings value and has quantifiable ROI
3. Build on your core competencies – picking up opportunities in an opportunistic manner leads to failure
4. Cutting prices is an extremely dangerous and costly way of procuring business. Don't try to buy low cost business unless you can turn around profitably in the medium term

A FAILURE'S REMINISCENCE
LESSONS FROM A LIFETIME OF MANAGEMENT BLUNDERS

Employee Selection – Focus on results

Talent acquisition is a challenging job. One is never sure how well one has done the job until the results become apparent over a period of time.

Having been involved in a fair bit of staffing globally, I generally come across managers demanding the best candidate for a position. What appears to be a great candidate to one person appears to be a hopeless candidate on the same panel. Most panels do not have a unanimous view of the candidate and the most logical interview decision is to drop a candidate. On the other hand, if the situation is desperate, then the lowest common denominator is accepted and brought on board.

Most job requirements are elaborate on job specification and candidate requirements. That is the explicit part of a job description. However well designed the selection process may be what works in an interview are the implicit requirements. The critical part is neither the job description nor the interview. It is the part in-between.

Recruitment folks' vet résumés keeping the job description and the manager's instructions in mind. They may or may not understand the business requirement and the actual role of the candidate vis-à-vis meeting the company's and team's overall objectives.

A FAILURE'S REMINISCENCE
LESSONS FROM A LIFETIME OF MANAGEMENT BLUNDERS

Many times managers prefer to speak to the candidate and make the determination rather than trust the recruiter with the information. What the recruiter looks for in a candidate is different from what the manager needs.

It helps reduce the number of interview cycles if the job description also mentions the key result areas for the candidate or even more specifically quantify the results expected from the candidate as a part of the role.

In a conventional interview, managers check the candidate for knowledge and experience. In an era where internet classes, interview questions and finishing schools abound a candidate determined to succeed will be well prepared to succeed.

When a recruiter starts an interview process with the end in mind and questions the candidate about the responsibilities and achievements from a perspective of his success in the current role, the numbers of persons who qualify reduce dramatically. The perspective of who is a good candidate or a bad candidate changes. The qualification moves to the person who is the best fit for the job. The most appropriate person is one who is able to deliver pre – determined results.

Execution is all about getting things done. Ability to execute needs to be cultivated over a period of time. Every person will come with the track record of having executed the

A FAILURE'S REMINISCENCE
LESSONS FROM A LIFETIME OF MANAGEMENT BLUNDERS

particular task or not. It follows that the most accomplished person may not necessarily be the right person for the role.

When the key result areas become the key focus of an interview, it is easy to quantify the achievements of a person in his existing job and previous roles. As long as the achievements are quantified, references checks cease to be subjective. An objective reference check, once the candidate puts in his papers in the current position, will both validate the interview claims and also bring to surface risks of hiring the person. A mitigation strategy is required to be drawn before the person comes on board to handle the apparent weakness in the individual.

The fact that organizations with six to seven levels of interviews still have a high level of attrition and employee professional dissatisfaction is anecdotal evidence that the present mode of interview should change.

LESSONS LEARNT

1. There is no such thing as a perfect candidate – what appears a good hire to one person may be viewed as a disaster by another.
2. Understand the implicit aspects of candidate selection – it is important to define the rejection, as it is to define the job description
3. Define the selected person's KRA very clearly in the job description – not the routine role description
4. Focus on achievement of the KRA in the selection process and not just on skills – the interviews must address if the candidate can meet our delivery expectations

A FAILURE'S REMINISCENCE
LESSONS FROM A LIFETIME OF MANAGEMENT BLUNDERS

People are not cost

Training and career enhancement are part of a company's responsibility to their employees. Training is management's prerogative. In most cases, training is suggested by the supervisor as a part of either the appraisal process or a reward scheme. In a few other organizations, people are requested to volunteer and training is allocated as per budget.

Normally, people don't ask for help in an organized manner. They may seek a peer intervention and help rather than walk up to the manager. This is even truer in a team where the manager lacks finesse. The other big fear people carry is the fear of failure. Admission of ignorance may imply lack of ability to work in certain places. A combination of reluctance to ask and fear of failure forces people to remain silent and under – deliver rather than ask for help.

The only way to help in such circumstances is to motivate by action. Setting unambiguous and clear goals, giving clear directions, training persons to deliver their piece, helping them get over problems and listening to their concerns are the five pillars of such motivation.

Companies are many time afraid to train people. They fear that people will learn and become competition. This is a short sighted approach since a person determined to succeed will seek success irrespective of lack of mentorship and training. They will move out in a short time and seek a real mentor.

In case you choose to mentor and train the youngster, don't remind about your investment in every meeting. If you have chosen to exercise caution during selection, and valued the person correctly, he understands the reason. Trying to buy loyalty through such reminders serve to do the very opposite of what you are trying to achieve - it makes the person lose self - respect and leave.

The process of a person's evaluation should begin at recruitment. People normally hesitate to spend enough time at that stage. They would prefer to take risks and move along. That is the beginning of the disaster. Grill on the person's career path and his route to reach the goals. If someone does not have a clue, he is a fit person to work for a government. A person with a clear goal and a path towards that goal is most likely to succeed. He would benefit more through your mentorship and your training. He is also more likely to stay the course and contribute to your success, if his path maps your own success path.

Before you give people goals to achieve, ask them for their opinion. It helps to seek their personal opinion about their own strengths and weakness to achieve the goal. A person who claims not to have any weakness has

A FAILURE'S REMINISCENCE
LESSONS FROM A LIFETIME OF MANAGEMENT BLUNDERS

either not understood the challenge or is prepared for it. The area of weakness is the place where you invest your training. Such training is appreciated, since it is of relevance. People who have nothing to learn are either candidates who should leave or the company should let go.

People are not cost and they should not be considered as one. Any investment you make in people will pay rich results if the training is focused to achieve the corporate goals and objectives. Budget focused training seldom achieves anything. Avoid pointing personal growth investment in formal meetings and informal get – together since that puts off people and encourages them to look out of the company. Focused people normally achieve corporate goals while stragglers spend time with the organization.

LESSONS LEARNT

1. Define your work profile in terms of achievement – let every employee know what specific objective to achieve before he leaves for home every single day
2. Define the process as clearly as possible – don't assume anything if you want a spotless delivery. Train on every specific aspects of delivery
3. Sit with the crew and identify targets collectively. Identify every aspect of weakness and that is the area where the employee needs training
4. Identify mentors in each team
5. Don't bring training costs in appraisal meetings. Every company trains to get better productivity

A FAILURE'S REMINISCENCE
LESSONS FROM A LIFETIME OF MANAGEMENT BLUNDERS

Endorsement pricing – A premium pricing strategy

Marketing books speak about four pricing strategies – bottom – up; sideways – in; top down; and dynamic. Each of these pricing strategies has appropriate applications.

"Bottom-up" strategy means aggregating costs and adding a profit margin to arrive at the price. "Sideways – in" is to study competitors pricing in the geography and determine selling price depending on the competition. "Top down" is to target an economic segment, determine the price and then engineer the product to meet the price point. "Dynamic" strategy is to use complex, real time information to reach the right price

All these models are extremely useful in a competitive market with well - defined features. However pricing aspirational, specialist or niche products is a different ball – game. In marketing aspirational products, one of the main challenges is to build a strong and invisible value to the product. The value comes from exclusivity and the aspiration comes from association.

Exclusivity comes either from exclusion or from association. The market for exclusion focused products is small in size and niche in focus. Association focused products are volume determined products that appeal to a well - defined segment of the society.

A FAILURE'S REMINISCENCE
LESSONS FROM A LIFETIME OF MANAGEMENT BLUNDERS

Products that are focused on exclusion target few customers over a large geographical area. Marketing costs are significant and pricing should consider the costs. In this case, it is mostly bottom – up strategy that works.

In cases of association, people who buy the product associate themselves with an ideal or cause or entity. The association could be a sporting team, celebrity, city or state, political association or social causes like environment, girl child etc. An endorsement in any form enables the buyer to contribute to the cause.

Any endorsement is but a story built around the ideal. More compelling the story, higher is the reach. The momentum so generated actually makes the cult association stronger. The product and idea both benefit from such association and each drive the other's growth. More compelling the association, higher will be the product price.

The association with the ideal has a larger than life meaning to the buyer. The product value is not directly derived from its function, but has a premium attached due to the association. The fair value for such product pricing is a factor of the total hype that is associated with the ideal and the ability of the person to pay.

Manufacturers of products that can address to a defined segment of the market create branding around a defined niche. They

A FAILURE'S REMINISCENCE
LESSONS FROM A LIFETIME OF MANAGEMENT BLUNDERS

associate the product to an idea or living style and build a compelling story around the product. Endorsements follow and availability is restricted to a few well defined places where the target market can identify. The audience pays a premium based on the economic profile and geography.

In mass products, it is normal for you to see announcements that promise a small part of the profits to a charity. That is one of the visible products of these endorsements. Celebrity endorsements, charity endorsements, cause - focused endorsements can all be priced in similar fashion.

If in a product space, more than one company display similar strategy, then the product category will mean to have moved from endorsement to a competitive model. In a competitive environment, marketing pricing strategy reverts to conventional model. Customers seldom give pay a premium for competing products.

LESSONS LEARNT

1. When pricing premium products, it is necessary to build a strong & invisible product value
2. In products focused on exclusion, bottom – up strategy works
3. Any endorsement strategy is driven by an aspiration. Stronger the association, higher the market penetration. Each drive other's growth. Pricing is normally driven by ability to pay
4. In mass products, charity endorsements bring relative product visibility

A FAILURE'S REMINISCENCE
LESSONS FROM A LIFETIME OF MANAGEMENT BLUNDERS

People Need Honest Feedback

Criticism seems natural, if you are the boss. Many bosses seldom acknowledge the good work that teams do. Many more believe that achievements are par on course and any recognition may come to haunt at the time of appraisals or even more sadly, the person may drop by and ask for a hike.

People deserve praise. They are extremely hungry for that. A regular pat on the back for a work done well is a strong motivation for better performance. If the praise is shared in front of the whole team or even by email, it is even better. A successful is a person who has sent at least a couple of such emails a day – it is, of course, more difficult to appreciate another persons' effort than it is to criticize.

It may not be a bad idea to send thank-you or appreciation note to the concerned person or team. In the past, I have ensured that teams have thank-you notes available in the vicinity and have rewarded persons who recognize others in the team routinely. That is a great way to bring teams together. Most people are smart to know the difference between a compliment, sarcasm and flattery.

While people are happy with a compliment, they are hungrier for honest and useful feedback. When a supervisor or manager takes time to tell a person about both the positive and negative aspect of the performance, it helps build a trusting environment.

A feedback session can happen over lunch, a cup of coffee, driving out on calls or while waiting for the elevator. The positive feedback is best given in a team meeting.

When a feedback is positive, it motivates a person to do better. When there is customer appreciation or a delivery happens under difficult circumstances or people go out of their way to deliver results or even if the work is flawless, an immediate pat on the back giving specific feedback makes everyone in the team understand what sets the tempo in the office.

People also take negative feedback under specific circumstances in a positive mode. If both persons are working to a common objective and if there is an instance where an aberration is pointed out, it helps the other person do course correction more easily. Comparing goals to achievement is another manner of giving feedback. If the manager has built a reputation for being partisan the other party needs time to accept the feedback.

Vague criticism or personal remarks are not feedbacks. A valid feedback is when you let the other person know where exactly the mistake is being done with an illustration. It is important that the whole process should be in a positive environment and without anger or frustration from either side. The feedback process is as informal as possible.

The illustration should necessarily show specific instances where the wrong is committed. The logical method to correct the mistake must also be explained, with a personal example, if possible.

If the mistake and correction is due to a process aberration, then the whole exercise must be recorded in a written format and added to the standard operating procedure after both persons agree that the suggested best practice is better than previously practiced working process. The importance of recording the event is to prevent the occurrence of the mistake by others working on the same process on a future date. The time delay between the discussion and documentation gives time to both persons to evaluate the problem and solution from an independent perspective.

In a world where companies have institutionalized incentives for people to do their daily work, the most obvious question is about monetizing feedback. Should positive feedback necessarily carry a financial reward? My own opinion is that if the feedback is anyway linked to an incentive programs, the feedback becomes a factor of budget. People hesitate to give feedback lest the budget overshoots. The feedback is by itself a reward.

LESSONS LEARNT

1. People are hungry for praise – everyone needs the motivation to succeed
2. Praise should be for a work done well – people can easily differentiate between sincere compliment, flattery and sarcasm
3. An useful feedback is something even more valued by an employee – the feedback must be honest and factual and must be useful
4. Vague criticism or personal remarks are not feedback

A FAILURE'S REMINISCENCE
LESSONS FROM A LIFETIME OF MANAGEMENT BLUNDERS

Make Competition work for you

Many executives are paranoid about competition. I have seen people who refuse to share sales presentations, lest the idea is stolen by someone else. In another case, the gentleman invited himself to my office and refused to go into details of his product till we signed the Non – Disclosure Agreement

Executives afraid that their concepts will be stolen are a mistaken lot. Core competencies take time to build. Track record and client respect takes even more time to happen. Anyone who can build a successful business based on a single presentation slide is a genius. No decision maker ever gets fooled by a slick presentation.

While most companies prefer to sell solo, teaming with competition is in many ways a success strategy. At the outset, the strategy may be akin to sharing the lion's dinner, but most times it works.

One of the pre-requisites of becoming a competitor's partner is to have an extremely strong and unique product offering. It must complement the solution that the other party is offering and must bring in strong customer interest. Every company can't master all competencies. The second and even more stronger reason is customer connect and track record. The track record must be demonstrable. The third reason will be size. Many government contracts have set aside.

A FAILURE'S REMINISCENCE
LESSONS FROM A LIFETIME OF MANAGEMENT BLUNDERS

Unlike what many people think, the set aside equation works only if the first two are relevant.

The second dimension to a successful teaming arrangement is that each team must respect the other team's credibility. If the equation starts with an assumption that the other party may steal a customer, this arrangement will never work. Any industry reputation for immature behaviour during contract execution or negotiation hampers teaming.

Any teaming arrangement may involve companies, but they are mostly teaming of key individuals to make things happen. Frequent changes in teaming partners or key negotiators retards the process.

In addition to the most obvious reason of getting business or quoting for contracts, a teaming arrangement happens for other reasons.

Large teaming contracts happen to reduce cost and improve economics of scale. We see such arrangement in the software, electronics, automobile and semi-conductor industry. In these arrangements, any company that is able to associate with major vendors drive the industry standard and ensure that RFP are tuned to the standard. It then becomes imperative for everyone to associate the company in its proposal.

A FAILURE'S REMINISCENCE
LESSONS FROM A LIFETIME OF MANAGEMENT BLUNDERS

In the consulting industry, we share resources and delivery capabilities. The default business model of most consulting companies is strategic association. Every company shares its niche competencies with others to complete a project. In this space, all are competitors and every one is a collaborator. Parliamentarians around the world are another breed that shares this competence. In politics there appears to be no permanent friends or enemies.

In construction, electronics and engineering industries, it is not uncommon for two discrete product manufacturers to design solutions revolving around products manufactured by competing products. Thousands of companies may contribute to the final product in an aircraft. Working on certain pre - determined engineering standard is a pre – requisite for this type of co – operation.

In the electronics space, we see that companies integrate a competitor's product in their solution and sell. In the integration space, the relationship happens both due to client's insistence on a brand and cost matrix of the solution or purely for relationship sake.

We have seen large retail store competitor products to justify the cost / square feet revenue targets. If customers like to shop for their requirement in a single store, it would seem foolish to stop them from coming since you don't a particular product.

In most aspects of life, collaboration is more suited for business than competition. It helps greatly if we can respect our competitor and see where we can benefit from their association, competence and track record.

LESSONS LEARNT

1. Teaming with competition helps many times
2. Teaming happens when the companies have complementary competencies and respect for each other
3. Track record is very important for both parties. When there is customer acknowledgement of competency, the mutual trust becomes stronger
4. In all teaming arrangements, the chemistry between key persons on either side is extremely important

A FAILURE'S REMINISCENCE
LESSONS FROM A LIFETIME OF MANAGEMENT BLUNDERS

Communicate to motivate

Many people communicate on a "need to know basis". This disease becomes extremely rampant as one move up the hierarchy. All information cannot be shared by everyone. However when an information affects a stakeholder, it is best to directly communicate the information rather than allow gossip mongers to take over.

The genesis of the information with-holding comes from the belief that it is needed to protect interests of the company. The genesis is always the person's insecurity. If a couple of peers at the top share this insecurity or feed on the insecurity then the whole organization responds to rumours actively and camps get formed in no time.

If a company's hierarchy is extremely rigid and unbending, it is very likely that people hide behind hierarchy to manage things. In those circumstances the hierarchy gives them power and information is the key to such power. This is second situation where information is with – held, since letting information flow dilutes the power.

In most situations, it is not necessary to pit people against each other to attain business goals. As long as the goals are clear, it is not difficult to communicate on a weekly basis the movement towards the goal. The key communication objective in this case is to let everyone know the big picture and the role each person plays specifically to achieve the goal. In an unorganized set-up, where managers thrive in anarchy, this will not be possible. When everyone in the team understands what they have to do, it is very normal for people to lend their shoulders to the task on hand. Project visibility makes even the otherwise laggard push, since the accountability is transparent.

Project visibility can be achieved in two ways – the first is internal communication and the second is visibility to a customer.

Internal communication in smaller teams is best done in a weekly team meeting and in a large or scattered teams, it is best done through emails or reports. If the reporting formats is simple and highlight achievements and failures then the report is normally accepted by everyone. A popular good practice is to source data from every team member and have that pooled together. Failures are apparent in every report and people understand if corrections have to be made. The organization as a whole benefits from such course correction.

Customer visibility always pushes people to deliver independently. It may not always be necessary or advisable for the paid customer to be involved in status meetings, but the customer hat can be worn either by a senior executive or people who are client facing and receive client frustrations

A FAILURE'S REMINISCENCE
LESSONS FROM A LIFETIME OF MANAGEMENT BLUNDERS

When stakeholders communicate progress and risks directly, all roadblocks to project completion gets highlighted. People in supervisory positions get lesser opportunities to play GOD or hide behind confusion. People will get frustrated fighting the system internally. With direct communication, bureaucracy reduces, and decisions get directly tracked to performance and achievement of results,
Everybody likes to know what is happening upstairs. The instinct is natural, since decisions has the power to both hurt and help the individual. When critical decisions are taken it is best to inform the entire team about the decision so misrepresentations can be few and far between. Seniors must be encouraged to deal with disagreements in meetings internally and all disengagements should not go out of the room.

If the transactions are essentially kept result focused and communications are channelized on client commitments and deliverables, miscommunication seldom happens. People get charged with the positive sentiments within the company and do not need external motivation sessions or internal team / boss management to succeed.

A FAILURE'S REMINISCENCE
LESSONS FROM A LIFETIME OF MANAGEMENT BLUNDERS

LESSONS LEARNT

1. Information must be seen as power that can be leveraged
2. Internal information sharing is best done informally and through reports / meetings etc
3. When there is transparency, fewer persons get an opportunity to play GOD. Misunderstanding is eliminated
4. Communication is always not necessary in a "Need to" manner

A FAILURE'S REMINISCENCE
LESSONS FROM A LIFETIME OF MANAGEMENT BLUNDERS

Complete today's work – avoid email

People appear to be always running behind schedule. A 24 hour day is seldom sufficient for many executives and knowledge workers. People work under extreme stress since timelines for most things appear insufficient. There is also frustration that progress is insufficient when the execution comes up for review. It is common to see people completely drain themselves before they are in their mid – thirties.

People who buck this trend practice a few common practices. The first and most important thing is to plan for tomorrow before you leave for the day. It always helps to have your last hour dedicated to plan the next day's achievements. Looking at the myriad commitments made during the process of the work gives us an opportunity to review and prioritize. "TO – DO" lists where all our commitments are listed ensure that we forget nothing. However small the task and however close the other person, getting an item into a "TO – DO" list means that we mean to achieve the task.

For many people, having a plan is an end by itself. They consider that their time management lessons well learnt. The real game is actually the execution. That is where most lessons need to be learnt.

A FAILURE'S REMINISCENCE
LESSONS FROM A LIFETIME OF MANAGEMENT BLUNDERS

Having a laser focus on achieving the planned objectives is the first goal. It should be the only goal for any professional. The first 90 minutes is the golden hour to achieve that. I normally get to office before my team to ensure that I can work in peace and complete most objectives before others come and keep me busy. Focus on moving the needle in the direction you have planned. If you can achieve 50% of what you set out to achieve in that golden hour, your customers, employees and all stakeholders see one happy person to work with and you will surprising have loads of time for your family.

To help meet our objectives, the first hurdle we need to get over is to remove all "urgent" or "important" directives. This can be from our bosses or customers or just about anyone. These urgent tasks are actually silent killers. Most operational issues resolve by themselves if we stopped taking ourselves too seriously and / or feel the need to put the record straight. 90% of these emails would have not originated if someone had to pay for emails. However, professional etiquette demands we answer everyone.

The one thing I have learnt is not to open email as soon as I get into the office. Switching off emails two hours before I get to bed is another effective life - saving strategy. This sentence may look a little archaic – picking up the phone and speaking to the person saves a lot of time and misunderstandings. It brings the human

A FAILURE'S REMINISCENCE
LESSONS FROM A LIFETIME OF MANAGEMENT BLUNDERS

touch and eliminates the impersonality that comes with email. Collecting data and / or composing an email are the biggest time killer, if there is any. Consider the time zones before you respond, though.

The other huge time bagger is the updates on social media sites. If you happen to open anyone of the sites during the day or choose to receive the updates on your phone, I can just sympathize. Switching off the apps from your phone is a good first step. Removing email updates on every reaction to someone's tweet or status update does not harm anyone. If you don't, the only person who may be losing a life is you.

Having a 20 minute status meeting an hour before you leave is another good practice. It helps to summarize your achievements with your team or even the boss and emphasizing the plans for the next day always brings in a perspective. Have walk in meetings and carry a book along to note points. That way, the meetings get completed in a jiffy and you get an overall perspective of what you have to achieve.

If you happen to be unlucky to report to a sadistic, control freak [I think 50% of the persons do], then your life becomes more bearable if you let the person know the achievement and also ensure that your plans go well with the other man's plans. You will be surprised that the late night update calls suddenly cease.

A FAILURE'S REMINISCENCE
LESSONS FROM A LIFETIME OF MANAGEMENT BLUNDERS

The bottom – line is "prepare for tomorrow – not for yesterday"

LESSONS LEARNT
1. Plan for tomorrow before you leave for the day
2. Put a "TO – DO" list every day and ensure that the list is prioritized every morning
3. Have a laser focus on the execution. Every item in your calendar / TO – DO must get completed before you open the inbox or have the daily meetings
4. Duck "extremely urgent" and "most important" activities from your bosses, if it can be helped. If you are organized, then such missives should be rare and not regular.
5. Most importantly, switch off your emails / phone atleast two hours before you hit the sack. That is extremely important to ensure that you have a productive day on the morrow.

The Challenge of reviews

It appears that reviews and meetings are the sole purpose of many a manager's life. I know managers who look forward to week-end review meetings as if their life depended on it. In a systemized, process driven organization, these reviews are taken much more seriously than others. The motto is that anything that can be reviewed shall be reviewed. This is of-course done in the name of perfection.

Reviews are important and there are no two opinions on that. What is a subject matter of debate are the periodicity and the purpose.

Reviews of every aspect of the process may be a bit of an over stretch. Anything that goes to the client or internal decision makers may need one level of peer review. The operating caveat for such an assumption is that you have hired appropriate people and they know the job.

If the process or the expectations is unclear or the person is untrained, there is ample justification for one or more levels of reviews. In a situation where the expectation is uncertain, a manager will serve better to clarify client assumptions rather than blindly spend time on the document. A training program is time better spent if the person is new to the job or is not qualified to deliver the task.

A FAILURE'S REMINISCENCE
LESSONS FROM A LIFETIME OF MANAGEMENT BLUNDERS

It happens many times that people would like others to review since they don't enjoy the task given to them by the Manager. The disinterest reflects in the attitude to work and the output. If the situation is a "one – time" exercise, you may not have much choice. If the situation is endemic, it may be necessary to help the manager streamline the activity and have someone else interested to do the job.

The key challenge before any manager is to determine if a particular review is required. Every planned review, other than performance and failure reviews, must be challenged and their requirement is to be questioned. Every review involves preparation time, unnecessary meetings and a huge wastage of time. It makes sense to ask the question – "why are we doing this"? and "what do we hope to get out of this meeting"? If logic says that people are equally or better productive without the meeting, it may be necessary to cancel or postpone the review meeting.

If it happens that you spend more than 1/8th of your time in review meetings, then it implies that you have skewed priorities. Identify all review meetings that you are a part of and ask yourself the question – does it help me meet organizational goals or the key result areas assigned to me. The bottom line is that every meeting that does not in any manner help you get an incentive or raise or would be considered in your

A FAILURE'S REMINISCENCE
LESSONS FROM A LIFETIME OF MANAGEMENT BLUNDERS

appraisal for promotion is time wasted. Each of these meetings beg the question – "what am I doing here"? Many a times, your manager conducts those meetings because his manager used to do the same before him. A frank discussion on how you can better contribute to your manager's promotion by doing away with the review meeting should help to have you opt out.

The content of the review material is another area which gives a large amount of information. These pre – meeting excel or word sheets take a long time to compile. If same information is being captured in more than one place and they do not help or have historically helped in either [1] know the project status; [2] helped identify bottlenecks / risks / failures; or [3] reduce costs or make life simpler, then it is most likely that the particular piece of information is redundant. Removing redundant data from review scope is another way to make things smoother and meetings end quicker.

All review meetings are best held 20 minutes before lunch or close of business. If people go adequately prepared to a meeting and if the manager can stick to an agreed review agenda, it is more likely that the meeting finishes as per plan. It is in everyone's best interest to not introduce any agenda item not associated with the object of the review in the meeting. The meetings lose relevance when all issues under the sun are discussed in random.

A FAILURE'S REMINISCENCE
LESSONS FROM A LIFETIME OF MANAGEMENT BLUNDERS

Present an alarm clock, if your manager does not bring one for a review meeting. He can't get a better present.

LESSONS LEARNT

1. Many reviews are not required and are a waste of time. Challenge every weekly / monthly review in your teams and ask if it is required
2. Only the information that goes to the client and your company Board needs review.
3. Set the internal client expectation clearly and train people adequately. Arm delivery folks to do their jobs well
4. Schedule all review meetings 20 minutes before lunch or just before folks leave for home. Work gets done faster
5. Avoid unplanned agenda in review meetings

A FAILURE'S REMINISCENCE
LESSONS FROM A LIFETIME OF MANAGEMENT BLUNDERS

Emotional aspect of support

In a globalized world, any hint of localization appears blasphemy. When companies, big, small and tiny are jostling each other to outsource and lower costs, this article may seem like an anomaly.

Essentially branding is all about how your customers look at you. The degree to which a customer identifies himself with the company, product and people represents the success of the brand itself. Many aspects may come into the process of shortlisting suppliers; People however give their business to vendors they like and trust.

People like to work with others very much like them. Over a period of time, either consciously or otherwise, companies build an organization ethos. The ethos reflects the thought process and mind-set of those who have started the organization and are working in the company for a period of time. The ethos represents the company and the brand. Such ethos and consecutive brand building can be either local to a small geography or global. Brands like Apple, Harvey Davidson, Microsoft and others represent the global evolution of such an ethos.

Decision makers like to think that customers tune into a company for a transaction. The transaction may be something as small as reporting a problem or making a payment.

A FAILURE'S REMINISCENCE
LESSONS FROM A LIFETIME OF MANAGEMENT BLUNDERS

Even sending out a reminder is a transaction. It appears that such transactions can be quantified easily and anyone who can perform the transaction can be made to deliver. Number of repeat calls or speed of resolution appears to be the determining factor in evaluating the vendor.

No two organizations enjoy similar ethos. Each company has its own mentors and its own experience to help it groom its corporate personality. It is difficult for a vendor company sitting in a strange land to emulate the ethos of the client and have each client facing representative replicate the brand personality. Most times, the vendor or their client facing representatives may not even be aware of the client's brand personality or the kind of customers they are expected to interact with and provide a solution for.

It happens that in most transaction based sub – contracting systems, cost is the sole driver for arriving at the transaction based model. When cost becomes the key driver, the vendor's approach to the business moves to delivering at the lowest value. The drivers that attract employees to a large settled corporation is different from those that join a transaction based business processing organization. The ethos and working style varies wildly.

The brand perception and the brand experience vary when the same customer interacts with the two different groups.

A FAILURE'S REMINISCENCE
LESSONS FROM A LIFETIME OF MANAGEMENT BLUNDERS

The difference in experience is because the emotional experience of the customer varies between the two differing kinds of people who populate the two eco-systems. From a mature brand, you expect to meet dignified people, much like you, who share your educational and social backgrounds. They talk your language and win your trust.

During the support phase, if the voice tonal is harsher, the language less sophisticated or the caller is aggressive; you get confusing messages about the organization. The brand perception changes subtly and relationship gets dis – oriented. The customer cannot phantom which set of employees represent the brand.

The customer who logs on to the company always expects something more than a transactional resolution. He expects an affirmation of his trust. He expects to meet and talk to someone like him. Even if the transactional relationship is satisfactory, if trust erodes, satisfaction levels come down.

Every manager needs to remember that the incremental cost saving through an outsourced deal is offset by large brand erosion. The biggest challenge he has to encounter is to reduce the dichotomy as far as possible. He has to provide the service sophistication without reducing the intensity of the emotional relationship with the client.

A FAILURE'S REMINISCENCE
LESSONS FROM A LIFETIME OF MANAGEMENT BLUNDERS

LESSONS LEARNT

1. People like to work with others like them – even when they outsource their business ½ way across the globe
2. All companies have an organizational ethos. The ethos is very powerful branding and attract people to the company
3. Customers expect this ethos to be on display in every transaction – vendors may not bring the ethos in practice
4. Cost can't be the driver in defining these sub contractual assignments. The small premium that is paid to a vendor with similar ethos is worth its weight in gold
5. Remember that every small tonal change has a large effect on the brand

A FAILURE'S REMINISCENCE
LESSONS FROM A LIFETIME OF MANAGEMENT BLUNDERS

Alternate business plans – reducing risk of closure

Statistically, 95% of the companies, started with bank loans, close within three years of their starting. Seeding a business is a bloody affair.

Every entrepreneur begins a business with some vision for himself and the company. The vision is formally documented into a business plan, if the person needs external funding. Any reasonable business plan includes the sales, delivery and funding plan with assumptions.

The real game changer is the assumptions. From an entrepreneur's perspective, the assumptions come from many sources. Some come from experience, some from discussions and most of them are from reading or common sense. When execution actually starts, the true intensity of these assumptions unfold.

What actually happens in any business plan and cash flow modelling is that the known devils are factored and a mitigation plan put in place. In reality, the show stoppers are very different from what you assumed earlier. At each stage of execution, the plan and its assumptions change.

What that necessarily means is that a business plan is at best a 'work – in – process" document. What you give the bank

A FAILURE'S REMINISCENCE
LESSONS FROM A LIFETIME OF MANAGEMENT BLUNDERS

or the investors is just an intention. It cannot be the actual execution path.

In a typical business cycle, the best of plans and intentions seem to have a tendency to derail. People encounter more failures than planned. They trip more often, even with all the grooming and experience their previous jobs and experience has given them. This is a reasonable journey for every experienced entrepreneur.

Every failure, if considered as knowledge gained at a cost, becomes valuable. It helps further refining of business plan and makes the assumptions and risks more explicit. It helps if the promoters list the learning in an organized manner and list mitigation strategies appropriately.

The problem actually appears when a person or team strongly believes in the invincibility or rigidity of the original business plan or investors blindly seek results based on the projections shared with them at the time of getting funds.

For many entrepreneurs, every change in plan represents a failure. It hurts their ego when they have to accept failure. In such a situation, they believe that they can make lost time by putting pressure on their team to deliver more and better. The pressure cooker situation is all set for explosion and implosion if not handled with care. Not only

A FAILURE'S REMINISCENCE
LESSONS FROM A LIFETIME OF MANAGEMENT BLUNDERS

the promoters, but every stakeholder in the system gets burnt in the process.

Where a team has an unfortunate experience of taking funds from an immature set of people who have no clue about the business or who have bought into unreasonable expectations, the business plan and its projections become the standard to hang the executive team. In this case, the promoters have to fight internal pressures as much as client pressures and it is just a matter of time before they hang in the boots.

The solution out of this crisis is always to have a set of alternate business plans. The alternate plan may use the infrastructure or the core competencies that are built for the initial plan and use the same skill sets to deliver a whole new product or solution to either existing or a new set of clients. If and when such plans are available, it becomes easier for entrepreneur to de – risk at appropriate time. A smooth transition to an alternate plan helps promoters to not announce failure loudly and hold their motivation and close colleagues together for a longer journey along the same path.

It is always good to discuss the alternate plan with investors. Many advisors think that this could be blasphemy. It is however not the case. Having an alternate plan does not indicate that you are planning to fail. It just announces that you have an insurance policy to ensure that the investors do not lose their

A FAILURE'S REMINISCENCE
LESSONS FROM A LIFETIME OF MANAGEMENT BLUNDERS

principal. Fire sale never gives investors a decent return on their money.

When such plans are discussed with investors, the terms of pulling out of the primary business plan must always be defined. A desperate investor should not pull the plug too early and allow for fair share of failures and learning. What is entrepreneurship without business hiccups?

LESSONS LEARNT

1. The real game changer in a business plan are the assumptions – the real show stoppers are very different from what our experience indicated
2. The second problem is the conviction of the team about the plan – teams take the plan a lot too seriously and look at the implementation failures from that perspective
3. Be careful to solicit funds from immature investors, who can use the original plan to hang you and the initiative – understand the plan as a guideline that is meant to be changed
4. Have an alternate plan that uses existing strengths and competencies. When your original plan fails, you have something more meaningful to run after
5. Define ahead of time, when you will use the parachute, so the investors are not surprised at the changes

A FAILURE'S REMINISCENCE
LESSONS FROM A LIFETIME OF MANAGEMENT BLUNDERS

Expensive locations drive you out of business

In retail, location is everything. Thumb rules that equates foot falls with conversions over rules all other business logic when it comes to location.

Brands fall within some broad client definition. However broad the definition, there are only few places where people within the brand profile segregate and shop at the same time. A big mall or the high street attracts a cosmopolitan crowd that may not actually mirror the exact profile. Random walk – in by such a crowd keeps the store busy without ringing the cash registers. There is no business justification for every retail outlet on the High Street to claim a premium, like it happens now.

In very few such places where client aggregation actually happens, all competing brands desire a presence. The location attracts a premium. Within no time, trans-national companies with bigger budgets come into the picture. Local managers of such companies, who have no investment pressures and have a lot to lose if impact is not visible to their corporate headquarter outbid all other players. Smart developers actually pit different companies into a blind bid to ensure that they get the most favourable deal for themselves.

A FAILURE'S REMINISCENCE
LESSONS FROM A LIFETIME OF MANAGEMENT BLUNDERS

Most trans – national companies make a mistake of comparing lease and rentals with the costs in their home markets. It appears a steal if a US company compares lease rentals in suburban NY with the rentals in a metropolitan city in South America, Asia or Africa. Initially the premium looks justifiable as a business investment in the country. However, any such premium limits the brand expansion since land developers get the message that the company is throwing around money. Most importantly it takes a longer time for profitability to follow.

Cost management overrules everything in the long run. Peaks and troughs of business can be better managed if costs are under control. Lease or rental costs can only be a percentage of sales. When we spend money in anticipation of revenue, the delta in costs between anticipated revenue and actual revenue can hardly be bridged. Until business actually justifies, having a large facility at a fancy prices hastens the end of the outlet.

In a new location, it is always best to estimate sales conservatively and assume that the actual sales will be a percentage of the estimate. The lease rentals should be pegged a couple of percentage points lesser than actual cost in a mature store. The estimated budget should be the cornerstone for the location. Working from this cost perspective typically involves intense negotiation, but the negotiator can typically negotiate leases from a totally different perspective to reduce the overall burden.

Developers would be open to consider higher advances in lieu of lower lease rentals or larger lease increases once in five years instead of an annual increase, if the party can commit for a longer duration contract. The downsizing risks can be reduced dramatically if the estimation is pessimistic and the location can actually promise a better foot fall.

In case the cash flow commitments do not justify the lease rentals, it is most prudent to take sensible steps to reduce the overall store area as early as possible. Possible brand erosion is a fear that inhibits many managers from taking this crucial decision. If delayed, the decision can cause the ultimate demise of the brand or the store.

Any decision to reduce the floor space can be accompanied by altering the store format to make it appear that there is a planned improvement in store presentation rather than emphasize the down – sizing.

While dedicated stores have an appeal of their own, for most small and medium brands or regional brands, stepping into a new location would be best done as a part of a larger retail format. That would reduce set – up costs dramatically and the money can be better spent on promotions and brand building.

A FAILURE'S REMINISCENCE
LESSONS FROM A LIFETIME OF MANAGEMENT BLUNDERS

Another preferred vehicle is to have a profit sharing arrangement with the landlord. This would also bring substantial pressure on the landlord to assure appropriate foot falls, which is always a selling point at the time of negotiating the lease, but can seldom be guaranteed. The landlord would then be more than happy to terminate, extend or alter the lease to the requirement of the business. Paying a percentage point extra over the normal lease cost in a mature store will still be justifiable in that circumstance.

LESSONS LEARNT

1. Cost profits matter in the final analysis – not customer walk-in
2. Don't compare the rentals with your company's home markets – evaluate from a perspective of whether the cost can be easily amortized through store sale in the premises
3. Always remember that lease has to be paid irrespective of whether money comes in or not – have that perspective when you negotiate lease
4. Negotiation strategies can change depending upon your cash flow perspective – never negotiate from the developer's perspective of the market
5. Taking smaller space, in – branding in bigger outlets, profit sharing, longer leases, higher advances and lower rentals are many strategies to manage an uncertain store location

A FAILURE'S REMINISCENCE
LESSONS FROM A LIFETIME OF MANAGEMENT BLUNDERS

Market Share and Profitability

Market share is every marketing professional's Holy Grail. Lifetimes are spent chasing this elusive mistress. "Relative market size" is the mantra of every sales manager.

What makes "relative market share" such a huge and popular focus across the world is the strength it brings to the organization in terms of marketing power and to manage prices.

It is a popular notion that more the market share, higher would be the dominance and it would automatically lead to larger profitability. This is actually a misnomer.

Higher market share just means that the operating management gets a chance to standardize processes and eliminate waste better. If the company can use technology and other innovative standardization methods, it would lead to better realization. A larger base and hence greater customer presence can help bring pressure on vendors to give larger discounts and reduce wastage. This would lead to better margins.

Many marketers dream of getting higher prices due to lesser organized competition is not always a realizable alternative. Beyond a point, customers choose to talk with their feet, if prices exceed their appreciation of value.

A FAILURE'S REMINISCENCE
LESSONS FROM A LIFETIME OF MANAGEMENT BLUNDERS

In a given situation, with everything else being even and there being no external force guiding the market [governmental intervention is a popular force in many industries], the profitability curve increases with market share up to a point. The tipping point would come when the relative market share reaches between 40% and 45%. When a company's relative market share goes beyond this figure, the profitability actually starts decreasing.

The reason for this dichotomy is not really hard to explain. Till a point, cost management works. Inefficiencies can be identified and managed. Every cost management best practice can be practiced. However, beyond that costs cannot be cut without affecting quality. There is a stage up to which managements can deliver and not beyond that.

External factors will start kicking in at this stage. There are two kinds of customers in every business – profitable and unprofitable. Profitable customers have the right delivery expectations and pay on time. They are a mature lot to deal with. Unprofitable customers are those who seek to milk the vendors dry, come up with unreasonable expectations, always complain and expect top management's intervention for every unreasonable whim, and most importantly seldom pay on time. The amount of management and sales team band width

A FAILURE'S REMINISCENCE
LESSONS FROM A LIFETIME OF MANAGEMENT BLUNDERS

required to manage these customers are disproportionate to the effect their business has on the bottom-line.

When the market share goes beyond the 40% or 45% mark, more number of unprofitable customers starts walking in through the door. Every competitor's worst customers now start patronizing the company.

You know your company is at the growth maturation curve, when your top and middle management spends time handling service and product problems. The second barometer is the number of attorneys employed by the company goes up dramatically. You're company starts having a collections' department or engages an external agency to start sending reminders to clients to make payments on time. The problem is acute when the head of such a collections department reporting directly to the CFO or CEO instead of the Marketing Head.

Managements think having a disproportionate number of bad customer's is a business hazard. It is never so. Choosing to work with a bad customer is a decision that managers take knowingly. Every such deal has ominous portents even at the time of early discussions. Bad customers make negotiations an elaborate process and try to squeeze every available avenue dry. Beyond a point dealing with such customers is asking for trouble.

A FAILURE'S REMINISCENCE
LESSONS FROM A LIFETIME OF MANAGEMENT BLUNDERS

It may initially appear a marketing waterloo to lose such a deal. It is however a long term victory to have your competitors work with such mavericks – the more they are straggled with bad customers, more your business remains sustainable.

The management's message to its marketing field force must always be to go for profitable and sustaining business – not to grow market share for its own sake.

LESSONS LEARNT

1. Higher market share has its advantages in terms of standardization and waste elimination
2. Absolute market share does not automatically mean larger profits
3. In the run – up to dominate markets, companies should understand the implication of growth on the delivery cost structure.
4. It may be more prudent to remain small and profitable, rather than become big and unmanageable
5. Beyond the 40% threshold, many unprofitable customers add to the matrix bringing down profitability. They also increase delivery risks and costs significantly

A FAILURE'S REMINISCENCE
LESSONS FROM A LIFETIME OF MANAGEMENT BLUNDERS

What works in cost cutting

When business environments become tough, the finance folks become the company saviours. Companies and managements suddenly recognize the benefits of being lean and begin cutting costs. While a uniform haircut works for the military, it seldom works for business.

Any company that identifies wastage during the boom seldom needs the haircut. It is however difficult to encourage thrift when revenues are flowing in. Thrift and cost management should be an evergreen mantra in every company.

When push comes to shove and managements / governments are forced to cost costs, it normally begins with a stated intention to cut a specified percentage of the cost. The cost cutting happens across the board and the most affected are the silent majority who either pack-up and leave or just manage to integrate into the system. Companies send out efficient contractors holding back inefficient management layers. In most cases, the ones to suffer are external stakeholders like contractors, vendors and clients. A short sighted cost management program normally makes external stakeholders vary of the company and encourages price bloating in mid and long term.

A FAILURE'S REMINISCENCE
LESSONS FROM A LIFETIME OF MANAGEMENT BLUNDERS

An ideal way to build a cost management program in place is to build a cost inventory in the first place. The finer the structure the better it becomes to manage. All cost components of such a library should be classified into three broad categories.

Any component of cost that goes into your direct product delivery is best left untouched. Unfortunately in most cases, this is the area that managers first examine to cut costs. Cutting any aspect of cost here severely endangers the ability of the company to deliver projects or remain competitive.

The message that is sent down the line is that the customer still comes first, despite the company squeezing on every financial aspect of business. It helps to identify alternatives to the engineering or service components of your business. The process of such identification is necessarily to reduce waste and build value, rather than cut cost. All process or material alternatives and vendor changes should go through stricter due diligence. In a publicized cost management initiative, officers with higher level of approval must be involved in any product related changes. Value engineering and changes thereof, done in moderate steps, is always easy to manage. It must necessarily be a part of a company's operating culture.

There are always fringe elements to a product / service. These are nice to have

A FAILURE'S REMINISCENCE
LESSONS FROM A LIFETIME OF MANAGEMENT BLUNDERS

features built to pamper customers or employees. These are called "auxiliary business deliverables". The absence of an auxiliary deliverable seldom affects the value or efficiency of the core product. These are areas where maximum cost reduction is possible. A cost management scenario is the best excuse for the engineering or delivery management to examine the relevance of every aspect of this deliverable. In many cases, value engineering methods give many alternatives to existing value component of the product. Alternatives can be freely examined and tried. The direct sales team and sales channels resist these changes normally. Their objections are to be handled with enthusiasm and understanding by the top management.

"Business luxuries" are the easiest place to cut costs. Any cutting of luxuries has to start from the top and not from bottom of the hierarchy. When executives' perks are cut, it sends a strong message that the company is serious about cost management. People are more prepared to take their share of pain if everyone in the company is doing it. It is difficult to ask only a section of the crowd to sacrifice, when others are having a party. Even among business luxuries, hygiene related cuts must come later than frills.

A FAILURE'S REMINISCENCE
LESSONS FROM A LIFETIME OF MANAGEMENT BLUNDERS

LESSONS LEARNT

1. Thrift should be practiced in a boom, as much during the tough times
2. Uniform haircuts work well for the military, and not well for a business
3. Build a cost inventory in the first place, keeping in mind the revenue impact of every cost item
4. Anything that touches delivery and customer experience should be attacked last
5. The most obvious thing to attack are the mid – management and senior management layers and structure. This holy cow is normally the last examined aspect of cost management anywhere

A FAILURE'S REMINISCENCE
LESSONS FROM A LIFETIME OF MANAGEMENT BLUNDERS

Executive freedom and customer excellence

Customers call for support, when they believe that they have a problem that they can't resolve by themselves. Customers relate to their vendor organization based on their brand impression and sales pitch. They expect results and a viable solution to their problem.

No two customers are same. No two problem calls are similar. Each situation is unique, even if problems appear similar, since support executives' deal with human beings.

All issues that people call about can be bifurcated into two broad parameters – [1] those that fall within the broad definition of the contract; and [2] those that are outside the pale of the legal relationship. Crank calls from deviants are not uncommon to anyone who manages a support centre and support for these unreasonable calls are not considered here.

Companies have converted support into a cost. For most companies, outsourcing support is the norm. If a person in some corner of the globe lifts the phone and answers parrot – like, it is considered support. Companies have more or less quantified the whole process and metrics around Turn - Around - Time [TAT], Repeat Calls or like define Service Level Agreements [SLA]. Escalations need to happen if clients

A FAILURE'S REMINISCENCE
LESSONS FROM A LIFETIME OF MANAGEMENT BLUNDERS

are not pleased. Many contracts specify a penalty associated with escalations. This means until someone is extremely aggressive or completely disillusioned the company does not get a feedback. To make matters worse, many a CRM software are designed to close cases automatically, after a fixed number of days, to decrease the load on the operators and make a better pitch to the company sales and marketing management. In such cases, the onus is on the customer to keep reminding the support staff that his problem is still unresolved. This is living hell to the customer.

When support is in – house, it happens that strict hierarchy is brought into play. The front – end executives, the vital cog between the company and the clients are given training in a fixed Q & A format. In some cases, the time to complete the calls is fixed. The executive can't spend more than a few minutes with a customer. The computer screen will help the operator read out answers, as long as the problem is already recorded. Executives are not expected to escalate the problem to the managers. In many cases, managers are in meetings with their bosses and do not have the time to take customer calls. You are asked to call back after sometime. For my life, I can't understand how anything can be more important to a person in a support role than to speak to a disgruntled client.

A FAILURE'S REMINISCENCE
LESSONS FROM A LIFETIME OF MANAGEMENT BLUNDERS

The most common reason why a client needs to speak to a manager is because the front line salesmen are not sufficiently armed to help the customer. If the problem is genuine, the person has to escalate to someone higher in the authority and seek concurrence to provide a solution. This takes time since the venerable executives may other responsibilities and not have sufficient time to address customer issues. The customer support team is unable to even commit a resolution until the authority comes back.

The de-facto reason of having a customer support team is to enable the customer have a pleasant customer experience. The experience translates to repeat sales, brand recall and references. While only one in every ten customers may refer another customer, nine out of ten customers actually talk about their bad brand experience. Having an immature customer support effort may hurt a company more than not having a customer support team at all. We still buy cheap foreign goods and dump them when they do not work.

It is bad enough to have a problem; it is worse for someone to tell you that you have a genuine issue, but the policy does not permit a resolution or the manager is busy to talk to you and hence a resolution is not possible.

When someone says that the company recognizes a problem exists, but company

A FAILURE'S REMINISCENCE
LESSONS FROM A LIFETIME OF MANAGEMENT BLUNDERS

policy hinders resolution, it means very clearly that the investors are paying insensitive individuals to demolish the organization.

Company policy is usually a diplomatic way of escaping out of a situation. When managers don't trust field persons, then this is a face saving excuse. It is not difficult for companies to identify common customer problems and arm their front line executives to grant the benefit of doubt to the customer. Immediate resolution solves 99% of the issues. Managers need to be aware that even if a resolution is given, but late, the brand suffers. Escalations, if at all, should be time bound and the front line executive must commit the time period for such resolution.

As long as the company does not judge the executive's performance from this perspective alone and allows individuals to err on the side of the customer, giving field representatives greater freedom ensures a relatively hassle-free time to the supervisors.

LESSONS LEARNT

1. In a support environment, front line executives are measured in terms of TAT or repeat calls. The focus shifts from helping customer to taking in more calls
2. Front – line executives can't deliver satisfaction in the absence of decision making environment – support sucks when the executive agrees with your situation, but won't or can't help
3. Nine out of ten customers talk about their bad client experiences

A FAILURE'S REMINISCENCE
LESSONS FROM A LIFETIME OF MANAGEMENT BLUNDERS

Local Manufacturing – Success in foreign markets

Companies look to expand abroad to expand markets. Internet age and better transportation has only made the process easier. The number of international transactions has increased multi-fold in the last decade. Firms that never looked beyond their own state at the start of this century have plans to look at the world market.

Two kinds of products usually sell in the global market. Niche products that are patent protected and huge user value have a global market. These products have a high entry barrier and it is not easy for local firms to introduce a "me – too" product.

The second set of products is retail products which have a big brand and huge funds backing it. These products sell on brand name basis. They may be a premium brand in the local market, but they have an aspiration value to the consumers.

A specialty product can afford to be manufactured at the home base and shipped on need basis. Customers, who buy these products, do not expect local production and are resigned to delayed support. Manufacturers advise stocking consumables, since it is not cost effective to import in small quantities. Niche products cost more to manufacture, sell and support. People who value the product are inclined to pay more for both the product and the support. Most goods do not qualify to be called specialty products.

Marketing retail products is extremely dicey. Tastes change depending on geography, price point, culture, religion and beliefs. Any successful idea or product range attracts local entrepreneurs to introduce a product that is equivalent in quality at lower price points. Their superior market and cultural knowledge makes it easy for them replicate and move faster.

Foreign firms fail most times because they tend to price the products with relation to their home markets. This pricing strategy inhibits the brand growth significantly and can't reach a majority of the target population. If transportation and taxes are added to these prices, then the brand appeal narrows down. Beyond a point, a "me – too" product with celebrity endorsement, but selling at a lower point will benefit from the stimulation in market demand.

Keeping an eye on costs and selling price is an essential success factor in foreign markets. It is not just the size of the country, but the reach of the population at viable price points that should decide the entry strategy

Product localization is a challenge all products face. The demand may not justify running separate manufacturing lines for a

A FAILURE'S REMINISCENCE
LESSONS FROM A LIFETIME OF MANAGEMENT BLUNDERS

particular geography. Introducing products that do not appeal to local tastes will not help. Till the break – even point is achieved and local production is justified, setting up manufacturing facilities does not make sense. This is an interesting situation decision makers' face.

One way out of this situation is to actually look to sub – contract production to small or mid – level partners with appropriate design and production controls. Sub-contractors would accept the strict product and cost monitoring, if there is an aspect of export and buy – back linked to meeting the quality and cost matrix. If Investors can be made to understand that there is complete company backing to the localization plan and product failure or short term volatility will not make them abandon the partner, then it is easy to build and operate dedicated manufacturing set-up.

The last critical issue is intellectual property protection. There are some countries that have stricter IP protection than others. The product localization partner can always be identified in a manufacturing hub that is close to the market and provides legal protection. All continents have one or more local groupings that accept tax – free or tax exempt imports within the local region.

The trick is to have a localization partner in a manufacturing hub that enjoys tax exemption and physical proximity with the largest

A FAILURE'S REMINISCENCE
LESSONS FROM A LIFETIME OF MANAGEMENT BLUNDERS

market in the region. This strategy assures better chances of retail success in a foreign market.

LESSONS LEARNT

1. Patent protected, niche products and retail products with big brand appeal are two kinds of products which can sell in global market
2. A speciality product can be manufactured from home base and people understand and wait for such products
3. Local tastes and pricing points are important for retail products
4. Local manufacture aids product localization and helps keep pricing in control. It can stimulate market demand
5. Sub contract with necessary IP protection and buy back clauses will help make the product initiation a success

A FAILURE'S REMINISCENCE
LESSONS FROM A LIFETIME OF MANAGEMENT BLUNDERS

Integrity & Business Practices

Integrity is a word that appears to be present on all websites. Customer delight or satisfaction and integrity are two "must – have" words in every company mission and vision statement.

Even while every company, big and small, speak about integrity, the number of business disputes has gone up steeply in courts around the world. It is every parent's wish that their child studies to be an attorney.

Integrity is an ability to "walk the talk". It is basically how you react when past decisions and assumptions fail. It is how you view a situation when the transaction is doomed for failure – monetarily or otherwise. If you can demonstrate courage to do what is right, rather than what is just profitable for that transaction, you display integrity.

Integrity can also be seen as meeting the customer's expectation to be fair and transparent. Customers give their business since they believe you are better at the job, than what they can deliver by themselves. The unspoken, but extremely strong understanding is that you will do everything to protect and further their interests. No one would like anyone else to take unfair advantage of their ignorance or trust. It is reasonable for any customer to ask to

A FAILURE'S REMINISCENCE
LESSONS FROM A LIFETIME OF MANAGEMENT BLUNDERS

demonstrate that you have protected their interest in the transaction.

When a vendor takes an antagonistic view of such expectations there is a rupture in relationship. It is in the company's best interest to demonstrate transparency and let the customer know how you have protected his interests. A mature organization and management team builds their business around doing the best for the client. The effort is demonstrated through the process and the results.

The process includes that the team is trained' to do the right things in the most logical and cost effective manner. They are trained to document every aspect of the business that is critical to establish claims when customer demands accountability. The result of compliance of such process is a customer presentation that proves that you have met your customer's reasonable expectations. The presentation could be a test report or any other document that removes mistrust.

Sharing information in an open and transparent manner does not mean hurting the organization in the process. It is not necessary to share all aspects of the process. Only the achievement of the customer's objective is what needs to be demonstrated. When someone feels that you have short changed them, you need to demonstrate the contrary.

A FAILURE'S REMINISCENCE
LESSONS FROM A LIFETIME OF MANAGEMENT BLUNDERS

Integrity – led business looks at a relationship from a long term perspective. It is bed rock on which mutual trust is built. Every transaction is to be successful for the relationship to sustain. If the business is not profitable, you have no business to enter into the transaction in the first place.

In business, some transactions can be loss – making. The reasons for such a loss are due to wrong assumptions or misplaced expectations. Defining expectations in a clear manner is another important aspect of integrity. Sales professionals choose to downplay aspects that they feel may discourage the prospect to place the order. They are betting on probability to ensure that a particular aspect of the transaction may not occur. Nailing all assumptions clearly at the beginning of the transaction is the best way forward. It may mean walking out of a few unfavourable transactions. It however solves many headaches. Clean transactions help everyone within the company focus on success, rather than spend all their office hours in fire-fighting customers or buy trouble.

In business reality, integrity is nothing but a mature way of doing business. Organizations everywhere choose to abandon maturity for extremely short term, transaction related loss avoidance or to assuage personal egos.

There is nothing wrong when managements want every transaction to yield profits. When teams enter business with that mind-set, the minimum they can do is to remove the word integrity from their websites and mission statements. Pursuing shareholder interests is no crime and that is what they have to advertise.

When companies have clarity on their objectives, customers have no business to expect transparency, fair and equitable business deals or business maturity. That is not a part of the deal.

LESSONS LEARNT

1. Integrity is about you react when past decisions and assumptions fail. It is about how you "walk the talk"
2. Transparency is another hallmark of integrity – more you communicate, the better it is
3. Defining expectations and also the exceptions in every transaction is important to retain customer expectations
4. Ensure that your sales guys don't bet on probability to beat delivery odds.
5. Integrity is basically a mature way of doing business

A FAILURE'S REMINISCENCE
LESSONS FROM A LIFETIME OF MANAGEMENT BLUNDERS

Founder Discord

When companies are formed, a lot of passion, dreams and trust are invested into the organization by all investors. This fraternity comes from mutual trust and respect in other person's competency.

Discords between founders can happen at any time.

In the first couple of months, people break relationships if personal chemistry or working styles do not complement each other. Passion and personal belief still remains in people and investments can be returned or retired in a mutually agreeable manner.

The toughest grind is when progress is slow between the third month and third year and investments keep flowing out. At this stage, all mistakes and mishaps that can happen actually happen and all revenue projections remain on the excel sheet and seldom shows as invoice. At this stage, failures dent people self – belief and other external pressures add to the stress of the founders. More than 90% companies fold at this stage, either because founders can't bring in more capital or don't agree on how to fund the business or their self – belief completely vanishes and daily pressures take a toll on relationships.

The situation is actually messy, if the company gets customers and revenues and the magic point of break – even point is

A FAILURE'S REMINISCENCE
LESSONS FROM A LIFETIME OF MANAGEMENT BLUNDERS

reached. At this stage, the founders should actually focus on bringing value and revenues to the company. What happens at this stage is that people who stuck during trials and tribulations start getting into discords on how to spend the funds generated. Short sighted investors who are in their first entrepreneurial venture after a fairly long career as an employee look to en-cash as fast as they can. Insecurities inhibit them from taking more risks than necessary. There would be others who see success as a big tonic and justify taking more risks to drive faster growth. The divergent physical and security needs of the founders pull the company in different directions.

Another situation where founder immaturity is tested is when the company earns some quick success in its days and then starts facing problems due to unfavourable economic situations. People with lesser risk appetite grow anxious since they find it difficult to manage failure. This is a typical scenario where investors have to decide whether to continue to invest through the bad cycle or exit strategically. Any small communication blunder in this situation can lead to violent disruption.

Stakeholders must have long discussions to determine the views, concerns and anxieties of all stakeholders. It may be possible that more risky decisions were taken in the past. The same persons who initiated many such decisions are hesitant to do what is right for

A FAILURE'S REMINISCENCE
LESSONS FROM A LIFETIME OF MANAGEMENT BLUNDERS

the company in a downturn. This is fairly common scenario. Over – riding legitimate concerns will force a part of the team to leave the organization. In all cases, where clash of approach rather than clash of interests is the reason of failure to bond, the separation will be long & dirty.

The other common reason for break – up once the brand is established is lack of communication. When companies are cash surplus, hierarchy and layers come up in no time. Loose talk or partisan behavior by the middle management personnel often leads to mistrust between the founders. The best thing for the founders to do is to sit together and trash out the issue. Egos help build communication walls and email becomes the preferred mode of communication. When company affairs are discussed by email, rather than in meetings, you know that company is on a downward relationship spiral. That is the beginning of the end.

In all situations where investors disagree, the golden rule is never to involve the organization. The conflict resolution has to happen outside of office in an environment of respect. Legitimate professional mistakes may have compounded the problem. The temptation to list or use the mistakes to question the credibility of the other person should always be avoided. In case, there is a serious lack of trust between the parties, it is better to start discussions with facts in hand, rather than with impressions. The financial figures or quantitative picture must be available to both parties. Everyone must agree that the data is trust worthy and the discussions should begin from that perspective. When discussion happens on basis of facts and not emotions, it is possible the situation resolves by itself.

One way to demonstrate mutual respect is to have an understanding that forces founders to communicate. The person who does not own responsibility for a function takes the final decision on an issue. That way the commercial guy takes a decision on a key technical aspect involving investment and a technical person may veto a commercial proposal.

If everything fails, the investors must decide to end the relationship in a manner that does not hurt the organization. The decision must be executed with mutual trust, decency and decorum that should not leave the organization in disarray.

LESSONS LEARNT

1. Founder discords start either because there is not sufficient fund generated by the business or because they don't agree on how to use the extra cash
2. Divergent security needs is another area of discord – whether to reinvest or cash out quickly
3. When founders communicate through email, hierarchy or relatives, and not directly, there is bound to be discord
4. When there is discord, the golden rule is to have a discussion outside the organization and resolve issues. In a healthy relationship, there is no issue that can't be resolved

A FAILURE'S REMINISCENCE
LESSONS FROM A LIFETIME OF MANAGEMENT BLUNDERS

Are Loyalty Schemes required?

Loyalty Cards or reward points are the new marketing magic bullet. Almost every organization in the business – to – customer space [B2C] space has some sort of loyalty reward scheme. The program started with airlines and retail. The idea is very popular today.

The concept of rewards began in the business – to – business space. Frequent purchasers and bulk purchasers got volume discounts and dealers and other intermediaries were part of schemes to incentivize sales. In a cluttered market, the schemes were meant to coax the retailer to push a particular product, in preference to others, for a consideration that was not necessarily linked to the commission that his employer enjoyed. It was thought that such interventions could help buy retailer loyalty. For all products, that involved counter sales and was transaction led, this was a sound tactical sales approach.

In a bid to hold on to existing customers, the reward point system appeared extremely sensible. Instead of spending budgets to attract new customers, spending a small part of the same money to retain existing clientele made eminent sense.

People give their business to companies they like or identify with. The most important aspect of retaining a customer is a positive

A FAILURE'S REMINISCENCE
LESSONS FROM A LIFETIME OF MANAGEMENT BLUNDERS

experience – not once, but every time. Clients who dislike the service or can't evaluate the value of a product from a price perspective move to competition.

Product loyalty evolves from the basics. The bottom – line is that a happy customer keeps coming back. At the basic level, it first involves getting the product / service to be of the highest level possible at that price point and then looking at extra allurements. If companies can demonstrate extra value for the money paid, then the chances of making a customer happy is much more than to manage with the minimum. The third part of the paradigm is to set the customer expectation realistically. Alluring advertisements or brochures with lofty claims would attract a customer, but would contribute to immediate and disproportionate disenchantment.

In every situation, where there is a human interface to product selling or service delivery, the buying and support experience would define if the client would remain loyal to the brand or not. Companies that outsource indiscriminately or build structures that are too aggressive or forget to train the field representatives are doing a huge disservice to their brand and the investors.

Indiscriminate outsourcing may come cheap, but when the service sucks, no one in their right minds would go back to the brand, if there is a reasonable alternative. When

A FAILURE'S REMINISCENCE
LESSONS FROM A LIFETIME OF MANAGEMENT BLUNDERS

institutions sent indiscriminate and constant payment reminders to conscientious customers, you force a good customer to move out. Parking hassles or inordinate waiting time at check – outs are experiences, that people carry and relate, and these put off the customer more than anything else.

Loyalty schemes are necessary only in those situations where direct company interface is low or product experience is beyond an organization's control. Very few organizations like companies that issue credit cards, some online portals and niche manufacturers qualify for such extreme situations.

Airlines, retail establishments and eateries are wasting investor's money issuing loyalty cards. The management should focus to make customer experience better rather than offer inane rewards for something the customer is habituated to do every day.

If an airline customer is budget focused, he will fly in the airline giving him the lowest price that evening. If a customer needs in – flight entertainment or food on board, he would possibly not prefer to fly a low cost airline. His choices are defined by his need. Most frequent fliers have their preferences that come from experience.

It makes more sense to build competencies that makes it more compelling for a customer to extend his patronage, rather than waste

A FAILURE'S REMINISCENCE
LESSONS FROM A LIFETIME OF MANAGEMENT BLUNDERS

money on schemes that does not add any value to the organization.

LESSONS LEARNT
1. Loyalty schemes was started to coax retailers to sell in a crowded B2B market
2. Product loyalty basics is – happy customers come back
3. We incentivise our clients to move out by not focusing on our product & service – clients don't move if we don't give them a chance
4. Build competencies that hold on to a customer, instead of throwing good money on loyalty schemes

A FAILURE'S REMINISCENCE
LESSONS FROM A LIFETIME OF MANAGEMENT BLUNDERS

Grading performances – does it make sense?

Performance appraisal is an annual ritual in most organizations. Organizations suddenly wake up to the potential of spread sheets during this ceremony. It is a great networking event and in many companies, managers meet their subordinates for the only time in a year.

It is necessary to evaluate performances. It is necessary not only for the organization, but also for the employee. Everyone likes to know what their boss feels about their performance. People are anxious get a feedback on possible areas of improvement if they respect the boss.

The most important reason why folks look forward to this event is because it is corporate equivalent of Christmas. In a talent scarce environment, managers are evaluated by their ability to give. When bosses speak to their subordinates about issues that include promotions and increments, the package includes areas of criticism. Everyone comes prepared for the package.

Managers learn that their budgets can afford only so much width and no more. It is quite obvious that everybody's greed cannot be managed. Companies can only provide inflation linked hikes to most employees. A manager has alternatives to share, if the package can't include a sumptuous hike. It

A FAILURE'S REMINISCENCE
LESSONS FROM A LIFETIME OF MANAGEMENT BLUNDERS

includes designation change, awards, promotions, a foreign assignment, shifts to a friendly team or even ESOPs. Quite obviously the person who complains the loudest gets more than others — that is law of the jungle and corporate evaluation process.

Performance evaluation is one of the several management tools that evolved with scientific management. The intent was that work study process would define "scientific targets". Metrics would help grade people and appraisal would be a welcome feedback loop.

The problem arises when the process gets adapted to knowledge management workers. Target definition is difficult or extremely opaque in most cases. People work according to the needs of the project or the whims of their bosses. Even in cases where some amount of repeatability can be observed, there are no scientific measurements to define an agreeable work standard. Historical track records may be an indicator, but not an absolute standard. There is no concept of return of investment on a person's time in many cases. Quality of service is an abstract concept when it cannot be measured. The process of defining quality is the bigger challenge in most scenarios.

In an ecosystem of personal relationships, blurred targets, dynamic work situations and undefined quality, the basic premise of measuring performance against a target and a standard is not there.

A FAILURE'S REMINISCENCE
LESSONS FROM A LIFETIME OF MANAGEMENT BLUNDERS

If managers have pre – determined targets to grade 15% of the persons as valuable; 15% as laggards; and the like, what the system allows for is only witch – hunting. The best 15% stand out any day and have choices. No company would like to disengage them until and unless the reporting manager has a sufficiently strong reason to disturb the status - quo. The rest are literally sized based on their ability to create a nuisance or blow a stink.

The current performance appraisal system and grading provides huge opportunities for all kinds of stereo-typing and can be easily used to discriminate people based on color, gender and whatever else is required to keep people out.

Performance appraisal and people grading as the sole basis of promotions and salary enhancements are probably an unkind basis for both the management and the employee. It can be a powerful tool to sensitize people on their drawbacks and identify areas of improvement. It is also possibly the best platform to get a feedback on the company, products and management direction. Everyone has a lot to learn in the process. Any other reason for its application causes more heartache and animosity than promoting a shared vision and execution.

Performance appraisal system and grading systems are the reason why the saying –

A FAILURE'S REMINISCENCE
LESSONS FROM A LIFETIME OF MANAGEMENT BLUNDERS

"people join organizations and leave due to their managers" appear apt.

LESSONS LEARNT

1. Annual appraisal is like a Christmas party – people come for the celebration, with the knowledge that fireworks as a part of the party
2. Performance appraisal, in the absence of scientific target definition or in an era of changing targets, is self-defeating
3. The popular practice of putting people in pre-determined performance baskets is even more hilarious – it encourages groupism and rewards people who complain loudest
4. It is best to delink appraisal and hikes
5. Use the appraisal to give formal performance feedback

A FAILURE'S REMINISCENCE
LESSONS FROM A LIFETIME OF MANAGEMENT BLUNDERS

Phone policy reflects personal values

Every interface with external stakeholders has a large effect on the brand equity. There is no substitute to personal experience. A pleasant personal experience has more than a normal positive influence and a negative experience will be a disaster.

At every level of phone interface, there are chances of negative perception being introduced. Each instance reflects on your perception about external stakeholders and your company's belief system. Stalkers and intruders must be kept away, but it is not always necessary to use sledge hammers, when a small pin can do a better job.

Companies routinely make you wait on phone when you call into their facility. Phones are not answered early or not at all. Even when someone picks the phone, they keep you on wait or disconnect without even the courtesy to understand why you are wasting time and money to call. The message that "we are too busy and please don't intrude into my time" does no one any good. Why have phones if you don't want anyone to reach you?

Busybodies at the reception who are interested to know the business of the caller and the relationship with the executive shout loud and clear the company's working atmosphere. If the company is suspicious and needs to hide its client facing executives,

A FAILURE'S REMINISCENCE
LESSONS FROM A LIFETIME OF MANAGEMENT BLUNDERS

there is a problem. I have come across executives defend their company by saying that they are shutting out intruders who waste time. If speaking to strangers calling into the company on business is intrusion, then one really needs to know the purpose of having the executive in the first place.

Certain people abhor speaking to external stakeholders. They avoid them at any cost. Receptionists always speak of junior executives spending time in meetings. I wonder what kind of meetings does someone junior in HR, Finance or Accounts attend through the day. Companies need to acknowledge these behavioural problems early. People may need help and individuals should be encouraged to get over their inhibitions. Individual traits have a tendency to send wrong images to other stakeholders and the world at large. I am aware of companies who overcharge certain clients, since their client's accounting personnel do not communicate invoice related problems in time and this delays their payment cycles. Word gets around that companies are unethical and don't pay on time due to these avoidable behaviour.

Companies introduce hoops when asked to speak to executives. Executive time is costly and there may be a need to rationalize the amount of time spent on unplanned work. There is however a method in which this is communicated to the callers.

A FAILURE'S REMINISCENCE
LESSONS FROM A LIFETIME OF MANAGEMENT BLUNDERS

Intrusive questioning by gate keepers indicates extreme immaturity. Assistants' transferring calls to someone junior without even understanding the purpose of the call is just rudeness. Executive Assistants indicating that their boss is always in meetings even after a number of calls indicates unprofessional and untrained office at work. Who would expect a senior and well paid executive to sleep in office? I simply fail to understand what prevents an executive to train his assistants to collect information about the purpose of the call and train them to screen and delegate. A simple reply indicating the next course of action brings out the professionalism in the organization loud and clear. The caller personal respect for the executive raises even when work does not fructify as planned.

The worst part of the whole story is that in most cases, the executive himself may be unaware that his personal staff is battering his image by their nauseating behaviour. Their behaviour unfortunately reflects on personal and corporate values.

Intimidation, interrogation or pure lies by his staff directly reflects on the executive. He comes across as uncouth to external stakeholders. No executive is expected to nurture jerks around him and in their fastidiousness to protect the boss, the junior assistants may make him look coarse.

A FAILURE'S REMINISCENCE
LESSONS FROM A LIFETIME OF MANAGEMENT BLUNDERS

Values are an aspect of how we view life. We value what is important to us and our goals. We ignore or not consider those aspects that do not help us reach goals. When executives do not receive calls or respond to messages, the loud message they are sending is that they do not care for you or your business. They come out as selfish. They demean themselves and advertise their weakness loud and clear.

Rudeness hurts the callers self - esteem and inner dignity. The distinction between controlled aggression and rudeness is a fine line, but presents a whole new meaning to a stranger calling into speak to the boss.

The worst promotion about an executive's capabilities is when his personal staff comes to believe that they are as important as and smarter than the boss. Their self-importance and discourtesy not only showcase the boss as incompetent, but the organization as inept and people working there as brutes.

A FAILURE'S REMINISCENCE
LESSONS FROM A LIFETIME OF MANAGEMENT BLUNDERS

LESSONS LEARNT

1. Your phone system reflect your brand in a large manner
2. If your reception bars clients from interfacing with your executives, the management has to ask the purpose the executive
3. Junior executives spending time in meetings and avoiding calls are behavioural problems and need to be identified early
4. Intrusive questioning by gate keepers demonstrates company immaturity
5. Gate keepers must be trained to solve problems, if the caller can't connect to anyone.
6. Don't let your team project you as a bully and insensitive soul. It kills your brand

A FAILURE'S REMINISCENCE
LESSONS FROM A LIFETIME OF MANAGEMENT BLUNDERS

Operationalize integrity

Too many companies believe that having integrity in their mission statements and fancy wall hangings is sufficient to operationalize the behaviour. For some others, integrity is just another process that needs object and process definition. If there is a matrix to define the goal and a process to map the progress, then the company is thought to run with integrity. Specialist consultants help companies define the integrity standard.

The text book definition of "Integrity" is the quality of being honest and having strong moral principles. The operation part is based on positive beliefs and values. Belief stems from experience. Experience is a consequence of all rewards and punishment that follows a particular action. It stems from collective memory of the individual and each individuals experience is different.

Evolving an organizational structure based on individual experience is a difficult task. It appears easy to define an end point and the means to reach the goal. However, the key is actually how every person reacts to an individual situation. Stakeholders judge every situation from their perspective of integrity and that is where challenge evolves and companies fail.

Despite everything that may appear inconsistent and dynamic, the actual

A FAILURE'S REMINISCENCE
LESSONS FROM A LIFETIME OF MANAGEMENT BLUNDERS

structure to building a strong ethical organizational DNA rests on some basic pillars.

The first pillar is the "reward and punishment" system that a company can devise focused on specific type of transactions. Defined behaviour that has a non – monetary incentive to deliver is the first step towards building specific behaviour patterns. Any deviation from such behaviour should attract a punishment that is more illustrative than painful. It helps if the basis of each decision is explained to each and every individual implementing such policies, so they understand the logic behind the decisions, reward and punishment structures. If the behaviour helps reduce friction at work place and enable an easier work day concerning other stakeholders, such behaviour will get implemented faster.

Building an ethics structure involves a maturity phase. Changes have to be identified and classified. Starting with low hanging fruits that are beneficial to all concerned help build enthusiasm and motivation for the project. Tougher tasks that involve corruption and slackness attract stronger reactions, but involve only a smaller section of the population. These have to be handled with care, but with greater organizational transparency. The effect deviant behaviour has on the well-being of every other active stakeholder, if explained with facts and figures will dispel any negativism on the shop floor.

A FAILURE'S REMINISCENCE
LESSONS FROM A LIFETIME OF MANAGEMENT BLUNDERS

The second key pillar is Trust. Trust is what defines how the front line person executes the plan. If there is a fear that his immediate supervisor has not bought into the company objectives, it becomes very difficult to implement the program. Individuals must be given the benefit of doubt, when they take decisions within the overall framework of the system. When respect and trust comes into the equation, it becomes easier to carry along the front line field personnel.

The third component is process visibility. Ethics explained in a common sense language is well appreciated. When process is simple and straight forward, the behavioural responses are suited to keep them simple. Working with tools like checklists helps to clear the maze and keep life simple. If the process is complicated and the execution team does not understand the method behind such complication, then corruption and smart behaviour starts. Ethics walks out of the door.

The fourth pillar is communication. There should be a forum where desired behaviour gets social recognition within the group and undesired behaviour generates strong negative group behaviour. Repeated management emphasis and training are two approaches that move the communication bandwagon towards the desired behaviour.

A FAILURE'S REMINISCENCE
LESSONS FROM A LIFETIME OF MANAGEMENT BLUNDERS

The fifth pillar revolves sensible management and investor expectations. Any exceptional behaviour and targets push people to compromise. Meeting extended targets involve certain aggression and push that may move the limit of tolerance beyond a point. In an otherwise equal and competitive world, average industry growth rates reflect the physical mean of achievements. Any growth more than twice the most aggressive competitor is a cause of concern.

The last but strongest pillar is the management behaviour. The way management behaves in an adverse situation determines the ethical measure of the organization. Any amount of hoardings, trainings, pep – talks and process improvement is a waste, if the company management is seen to practice short – cuts in business. Ceaser's wife has to be above board in more ways than one.

LESSONS LEARNT

1. Integrity is beyond object and process definition – it is about enabling behaviour
2. Operating part is all about positive beliefs and values
3. Individuals' have personal standards of integrity and that is the real challenge of institutionalizing integrity
4. Build a "reward & punishment" system for defined outcomes
5. Define outcomes and trust people to implement them – allow them scope to commit mistakes
6. Keep process simple and transparent
7. Desired behaviour should get social recognition
8. Keep expectations reasonable – immature targets motivates unethical behaviour

A FAILURE'S REMINISCENCE
LESSONS FROM A LIFETIME OF MANAGEMENT BLUNDERS

Is Recruiting a HR function?

Recruitment is an important part of every human relations syllabus. HR departments manage recruitment in most organizations, since the traditional belief that anything to do with human beings is a HR function.

Any aspect of business that involves human beings requires a set of skill sets that include patience and empathy. A Human Relations Executive by definition needs to be passive in approach, even if proactive in application. Any perception of hard selling or manipulation can kill trust that is so vital for the success of the role.

Recruiting, on the other hand, is basically a sales profession. You are targeting a prospect, either active or passive, hard selling the company and the role, convincing him to attend interviews on time, selling the reimbursement package and finally following up till the person actually comes on board. Aggression and dynamism are the two key skill sets that play an active role in the success of a head hunter. A "never – say – die" approach is what makes a large difference between a successful recruiter and a mediocre professional. Most successful recruiters, I have worked with, have an extremely out – going approach to life and never hesitate to pick the phone.

A FAILURE'S REMINISCENCE
LESSONS FROM A LIFETIME OF MANAGEMENT BLUNDERS

The basic character attributes to either profession is as different as chalk and cheese.

Good recruiters today have very little professional choice for career growth. Colleges and formal learning gives them an illusion that a HR profession is their preferred growth avenue. When they step into the role, frustration awaits them. Like every other sales person, the attention span of these individuals is extremely small. The joy and success that propelled them into the current designation beats them hallow. The focus on numbers that should be natural for a good recruiter is almost an alien approach for a staff executive. Pushing a number oriented sales executive lead a human relations team is more or less a disaster.

Most HR Executives are not comfortable doing recruitment. If the person is given a large active database to hunt, the frustration may not become so evident. The frustration shows especially when the volumes are high and position is extremely specific. The possibility of such people doing head hunting, cold calling into companies and convincing a person to send his résumé is very bleak. If the position requires that the customer vets the résumé and hiring decisions are based on the whims and fancy of the hiring manager, then inevitably a head hunting agency gets a contract.

A FAILURE'S REMINISCENCE
LESSONS FROM A LIFETIME OF MANAGEMENT BLUNDERS

Companies have to be careful hiring persons for either job. If the job requires sporadic internal hiring, a HR executive with a proactive attitude would be able to do complete justice to the job. If recruitment requirement is large and / or requires customer clearance / interviews for approval, then a full time recruitment person would be preferable.

The career path for a recruiter is as a business manager or an account executive with the client and not as a HR Manager. A good recruiter would be very successful sales person, if you are not a staffing company. On the other hand, every HR executive is a staff person. Managing personnel, statutory filing and administration would be the scope of what they would do. Their growth prospects are along parallel lines to a recruiter.

LESSONS LEARNT

1. Human relations role requires passive approach and proactive application
2. Recruitment is a sales activity – the role requires an aggressive approach to business with active metrics related outcomes
3. Recruiters have no logical career progression – they would be a failure as a HR professional
4. Recruiters grow better as account managers or business executives

A FAILURE'S REMINISCENCE
LESSONS FROM A LIFETIME OF MANAGEMENT BLUNDERS

Should Exit Plan be Part of Business Plan?

Entrepreneurs start company to make money. They also start a company to execute a passion. If there is no passion in the business, the company never takes off anyway.

One of the critical tools for any start – up looking for capital is the business plan. Business plans are a must, even otherwise. They help founders define the growth path of the organization. The plan helps organizations seize opportunities, define risks and also modulate execution.

The last slide of any business plan is the exit strategy. Exit strategies is manner of speaking, the founders understanding of who will buy the business after a period of time.

In recent times, it has become fashionable for founders to speak about selling their companies over a three year to five year horizon to a larger setup. Some plan retirements even before the ink on the business plan dries up. New companies speak about listing their organizations within a couple of years and others promise employees the moon by sharing equity and the planned listing. Unsurprisingly, many entrepreneurs, I speak with, buy this tale about retirement and management luxury quite seriously. That is their excuse to take risk and start a company in the first place.

A FAILURE'S REMINISCENCE
LESSONS FROM A LIFETIME OF MANAGEMENT BLUNDERS

There is nothing wrong in thinking big and working to make an impact. The problem actually is that less than a percent of companies actually survive to be acquired and less than a percentage of companies that survive are listed and even fewer founders actually become billionaires. It is fascinating to read about the billions a few kids have made in the market, but we seldom advertise the blood bath in the start-up space in equal measure.

When the reality is so sullen, why do we still so enthusiastically define the exit plan? Is the exit plan really a necessity?

An entrepreneur completely driven by an idea would need to completely devote his all if he has to succeed. The harsh reality of running a start – up is that you sacrifice regular salary, benefits, holidays and even peace of mind to execute a journey you strongly believe in. The journey is lonely and most often a wasted effort.

If the person enjoys the journey, he is blessed. He may not want the journey to end. Even a billion would not enthuse him to sell, since he knows that life would not be better in any other way. Such a person spends all his waking time making a difference and all his sleeping time planning to work better. The differentiator is absolutely the scale and perfection that the founders have built into

A FAILURE'S REMINISCENCE
LESSONS FROM A LIFETIME OF MANAGEMENT BLUNDERS

the DNA. These are businesses that venture capitalists would like to acquire.

If the business has a strong foundation and an excellent delivery structure, you would expect it to be profitable and cash positive. Passionate entrepreneurs would not want to risk buying headache by way of an investor. They would rather build the business in an organic manner.

On the other hand, businesses find it difficult to grow beyond a point, if they have no differentiation or are not extremely specialized. They make some money and survive. Their journey is predictable. They are not the kind of companies that set a market on fire. These companies need money to grow. The investors look to lock in their capital, only if they have a special reason to do so.

For these founders, the struggle is initially to get an investor interested to sit through the entire presentation. Exit strategy comes at the very end. Most organizations follow this path and struggle continues. In this scenario, an exit strategy has no meaning till the founders' interest an investor to sign the check.

What can change for most companies is the nature of the external investor. If the external investors bring in more than just capital to the table, these companies have a capability to take off. The additional

A FAILURE'S REMINISCENCE
LESSONS FROM A LIFETIME OF MANAGEMENT BLUNDERS

marketing or client acquisition or management push benefits the organization and propels the delivery mechanism to the next logical level. At this stage of the journey, it is possible that someone may be interested in buying the organization, especially if the core competencies are strong enough to attract an investor. An exit strategy makes sense to the founders and investors at this stage.

The jury is out of on the issue of exit strategies. It does not harm or hurt to indulge in some idle fantasies. The founders however can do better to build a great delivery and sales organization. The exit knocks on the door.

LESSONS LEARNT

1. To "begin with end in mind" may be a great time management jargon, business organizations don't necessarily need an exit
2. If Founders build an amazing delivery and sales organization, and if business model is scalable, then cash profits follow
3. If organization is in a sufficiently large niche and is cash positive, then investors will come knocking. If it is a "me – too" business, no one will be interested
4. Entrepreneurs must ask if they need external investors to dictate the agenda. If they can plan organic growth, then it may be wise to keep off investors
5. Founder starting with an intention to retire in a 3 – 5 year span seldom build lasting business that would make them billionaires

www.ingramcontent.com/pod-product-compliance
Lightning Source LLC
Chambersburg PA
CBHW062350220526
45472CB00008B/1764